GOLD MINING

Gold Mining

Parenting an Excellent Child

By
TOSIN OKE

Copyright © 2022 by Tosin Oke
Gold Mining - Parenting an Excellent Child
All rights reserved

Dedication

I dedicate this book to the loving memory of my darling Pastor Nomthi Odukoya. I was looking forward to you writing the 'foreword' of this book, and to developing my relationship with you after reading your response to my Instagram message. Like a good student, I adapted your teaching style into this book with countless real-life stories. I trust you will be proud of me when every parent that encounters this book encounters a change in mindset. Rest on!

I also dedicate the book to every parent who desires excellence in the totality of their child's spirit, soul, and body.

Lots of Love!

Acknowledgements

Thanks be to God who gave me the courage, bravery, wisdom, and life to put this book together. I owe my life to you Lord, use as You please.

I am indebted to my family members; you are my greatest assets. A special thanks to my dear husband, Lanre Oke, and my precious daughters, Okikioluwa and Enioluwa. Thanks for being very understanding and loving me despite me. To my parents, Felix and Anthonia Pelemo – thank you for the right foundations. Anu, thanks for the childhood memories, Funmi, - thank you for being constant and for believing in me.

To my pastors 'Reverend Lekan and Pastor Dayo Fasina', I am indebted to you for constantly parenting and pushing mto excel in every sphere of life. Pastor Dayo, I specially cannot thank you enough for proofreading and guiding all the way.

I also want to express my heartfelt gratitude to the ministries of Pastor E.A. Adeboye, Bishop O. Oyedepo, Pastor Taiwo Odukoya, Bishop T.D. Jakes, Joyce Meyer, and Pastor Segun Coker who have been sources of tremendous blessing to my life especially during my silent chapters. God bless you more.

I certainly have to acknowledge Toni Daramola (co-founder of Blissful), who not only challenged me to write this book but encouraged me further by sending me a book and writing plan (in the UK) all the way from Canada. Thank you Toni-Dars for seeing what I didn't see ahead of time, and for pointing me towards God's direction at this season of my life.

Finally, my gratitude goes to the editor for being constantly positive and delivering to time.

CONTENTS

Foreword 1
Preface 3
Introduction 5
Chapter 1: Parenting and Preparing your child for Excellence 7
Chapter 2: Understanding Child Psychology and Development 14
Chapter 3: Seasons to be Mindful for in Parenting for Excellence 19
Chapter 4: Your Child's Spirit 38
Chapter 5: Total Mining 48
Conclusion 66
Further Resources 67
Contact Us 67
References 68
Book Review 70
Editor's Remarks 71

List of Figures and Tables

Figure 2.1: Stages of Prenatal Development 15
Figure 3.1: The Key Components of Erikson's Model of Human Development ... 19
Figure 3.2: The Key Ares of Development 20
Table 3.1: Erikson's Psychosocial Stages: A Summary Chart 21

FOREWORD

In the past five years, I along with my wife and some vision partners have focused on helping young married couples navigate married life and be their best as they pursue their forever after through the Blissful Group for Married Couples. This journey has brought me and my wife in contact with hundreds of married couples directly and many more through trainings, ministrations, and marriage coaching.

I am also honoured to have walked the talk for 11 years with my wife and watched my parents who are also seasoned marriage counsellors of over 30 years lay the foundation I now build on. This heritage and mission to see married people thrive places me in a vantage position to know how vital this book you hold in your hands (or in a device) can be.

I met Tosin through her sweetheart 'Lanre' about five years ago. Lanre and I were colleagues at the time. We quickly forged a very close relationship as we discovered that we were aligned in faith, principles, and values. Our families today have become close family friends and vision partners in Blissful group.

Tosin was invited to take a session on parenting in the group a couple of years ago; the session resonated so deeply, and the feedback was overwhelmingly positive. Till date the session remains one of the most impactful sessions we've had. It was imperative that the talk session be developed into a more accessible format. I nudged Tosin to act on this and you can imagine my joy on seeing that this book finally come to life.

Gold Mining is a resource that was needed before 9 years ago when my mini me was born and the next best time is now, when I can take audit and re-calibrate the parenting engine. This is a deeply insightful read that immediately lays out the parenting map for you. It starts out with a quick breakdown of the keywords and concepts and then lays a biblical foundation for your role as a parent. It expounds on the child psychological and developmental journey through the prenatal stages, infancy, pre-school, and school age until puberty, as well as what your roles are for each stage.

The material also emphasizes the place of spiritual growth in your children. Tosin has borne her heart out in this piece and even displayed vulnerability, sharing deep personal stories where it mattered to drive home key points. I personally find these areas the most compelling; it left me wanting to take more concrete and immediate action. This book will also provoke us to be intentional in stimulating growth in areas we are otherwise wired to leave to chance.

Tosin has brought her years of professional experience in childcare and international education to provide a detailed resource you can run with. She has also written from her rich personal experience as a mother of two multitalented girls (for now, as She and Lanre still owe the grandparents and us committee of friends at least one more girl or boy). If you know Okiki and Eni well, you will know she is walking the talk, and doing it excellently well. I do not know anyone more perfectly suited to write this book.

Parenting can feel like an extreme sport where uncertainty looms with every twist and turn. I know this because of my personal journey and my work with several couples. This makes this material a must-read for anyone wanting clarity on what they need to do and when to do it. It is a material I highly recommend at each stage of the parental journey and a reference material you need to have handy if you are serious about mining the Gold in your kids. I know this book will answer the quiet questions in the hearts of first-time parents who are uncertain and veteran parents who are looking for new answers.

Welcome to the Gold Mine, let's start digging!

— **Oluwatoni Daramola**
Co-Visioner, Blissful Group for Married Couples

PREFACE

A desire for children's wellbeing inspired the creation of this book. It is based on lessons learnt from parents who have successfully trained, prepared, and equipped their children, and from my personal reflections and experience. I believe everyone deserves to have the insights I've been exposed to, and that those who already have it need to be continually reminded to act on what they readily know. The book's title came to be when I had the honour of speaking to a group of couples on the topic "preparing your child for excellence" on a virtual platform called "Blissful." The audience desired a printout or document they could always refer to after the presentation and one of the group's co-founders subsequently challenged me to write this book. Members of the group who were affiliated to other groups invited me to speak as well, here I had similar requests, hence this present matter **'Gold Mining'**.

While there is no roadmap to raising a child, through the reaction of my audience and my work with children, I have identified that there is a gap to be filled and I recognise that my role in filling this gap goes beyond speaking at invited meetings and lectures to reach a larger audience. It is my hope that my insights and experiences will provide the necessary guidance in the "Gold Mining" of the next generation.

INTRODUCTION

This book contains information that will reinforce previous knowledge on parenting possibly from books, tapes, hearsay, other parents or peers, etc, in order to provoke us to do better by our children and wards. The purpose of this book *Gold Mining* is not only to share a collection of inspiring truths I have collated, which are useful for empowering our children for life, but also to justify why 'Childhood' plays such an important role in the course of the rest of life.

The insights in this book might prove daunting to apply but nothing good comes easy. Also know that it is not unusual for you to make unavoidable parenting mistakes, but it is in your power to keep striving for excellence and balance.

Some researchers suggest that babies are born blank, and that it is their environment that begins to fill that blankness with several elements that the children soak up consciously and unconsciously. At this tender and sensitive stage when children are soaking things up, it is important that grown-ups in the life of a child deliberately prepare by putting in place structures and boundaries which is pivotal to mining the gold in children, in essence, preparing them for excellence.

A child has the best chance to reach their full potential with proper care and stimulation. The action of gold mining with regards to parenting is parallel to stimulation. Stimulation is an essential nourishment that a child needs to develop excellence. It's not the quantity but the quality of stimulation that matters. In the western world, most early year settings and nursery schools provide lots of stimulation that create new experiences. In contrast, such provisions are not readily available in developing countries. Therefore you need to seize the moment in your child's early years and stimulate the golden substances in them accordingly.

I have compiled knowledge from diverse resources, as well as my experience as a UK BTEC Trainer for childcare. I've learned from pursuing an international degree that I must provide solid evidence to support all of my claims. I find this biblical because the scripture says in Matthew 18:16,

> 'But if he will not hear, take with you one or two more, that **by the mouth of two or three witnesses every word may be established.**'

In consequence, I will be citing some theories and publications to support my statements in the book. Although most of my parenting experiences are founded in the United Kingdom, materials quoted in this book were sourced from across the world.

The first chapter reiterates the purpose of the book and the importance of preparing the child for excellence. It briefly discusses the tripartite being of the child and introduces the critical times in a child's life in order to understand how to fully maximise the different seasons of a child's life. Chapter 2 helps to understand child psychology and provides an overview of what is required of parents to prepare children from the womb. The third chapter then begins to disclose critical times for equipping the child. It dwells more on the soul than other parts as it is the battle ground of every individual. This is also deliberate because it's mostly natural that parents equip the child's body with food, shelter, and clothing, then give little regard to the child's soul (will and emotions) other than the intellect. Chapter 4 is a sensitive chapter as it deals with the spiritual preparation of the child. Chapter 5 encapsulates total mining, providing ten in-depth habits that should be inculcated for gold mining.

Enjoy!

CHAPTER 1

Parenting and Preparing your child for Excellence

To provide a better grasp of the insights in this book, here are some definitions on the keywords from the title of this book and chapter.

Child

A child can be a little one, boy, girl, new-born, infant, toddler, schoolboy, schoolgirl, teen, adolescent, teenager, youth, young man, young woman, young adult, son, daughter, descendant, or offspring.

Legally, a child is anyone below the age of 18, however the Merriam-Webster Dictionary defines a **child** as 'a young person especially between infancy and puberty'. Meanwhile, according to the website of the UK National Health Services (NHS) and Education, ages 11 to 12 are regarded as the average age for puberty in both boys and girls, implying that a child is a person between age 0 to 12. The NHS further divides the stages of childhood within this age range as early childhood and middle childhood.

Whilst the legal terms of a child provides a limit, the scientific, cultural, and most importantly, human definition of a child is based solely on the responsibility of a parent to an offspring. This could be a daughter or a son, irrespective of the age. Hence, with parenting, there are no rules to definition of a child, and not even age should stand as a barrier.

Excellence

Excellence refers to the quality of being outstanding or extremely good. Excellence includes quality in physical, spiritual, emotional, social, and intellectual aspects of life. Similar words to excellence include distinction, high quality, brilliance, sand greatness, supremacy, worth, genius, accomplishment, expertness, mastery, and prowess. Some opposite words for excellence are inferiority and mediocrity.

The word excellence is linked to the Greek word 'arete'. To the Greeks, it is the ultimate expression of human greatness—moral, physical, spiritual. It is a person's 'full realization of potential or inherent function.'

Prepare

The Oxford English Dictionary describes the word 'prepare' as *making (someone) ready or able to do or deal with something*. Some synonyms for the verb 'prepare' include to 'gird up one's loins, arm oneself, train, get into shape, get set, do homework, instruct, teach, educate, coach, tutor, inculcate, groom, discipline, guide, direct, put in the picture, make ready, strengthen, fortify.

Gold

The Cambridge English dictionary describes Gold as '*a chemical element that is a valuable, shiny, yellow metal used to make coins and jewellery*'. There are countless values attached to gold. These include money, wealth, wherewithal, means, assets, resources, reserves, opulence, property, treasure, affluence, substance, prosperity, etc. I daresay, that a child can be likened to one's treasure, assets, reserve, opulence, and much more. For some people, their children serve as their retirement (investment) plan.

Mining

According to the Cambridge English Dictionary, mining is 'the industry or activity of removing substances such as coal or metal from the ground by digging'. It involves digging out substances that matter - they either matter because they are valuable to their original location or when dug out of that location. The nouns 'industry' and 'activity' also depict actions taking place. This suggests that anyone that wants to mine gold must be ready to act to dig it out.

Another definition of mining I find interesting is Merriam-Webster's. There, mining is referred to as 'the activity or process of searching through large amounts of information for specific data or patterns.' This implies that mining is a process that requires time. It entails consistency, requires you to search and scrape through surfaces until you get the gold you desire.

I usually do not like to source information from Wikipedia because once logged in on their site, anyone could edit information with limited restrictions and vetting. However, I cannot but cite Wikipedia's definition of mining. It elaborates the definition given by the Cambridge English Dictionary and Merriam Webster Dictionary. Wikipedia provided the following discussion for mining:

> 'Mining is the extraction of valuable minerals or other geological materials from the Earth, usually from an ore body, lode, vein, seam, reef, or placer deposit. Exploitation of these deposits for raw material is based on the economic viability of investing in the equipment, labour, and energy required to extract, refine, and transport the materials found at the mine to manufacturers who can use the materials.'

This definition suggests that you don't just dig out the valuable substances and leave them in their original form, you also need to refine these materials by investing in resources required to bring them into their best shape or form (gold).

The definitions from the three sources use the verbs 'search, extract, remove, exploit'. Although these definitions don't disclose *when* the actions (verbs) should be done, they encompass the What, How, Where, and Why mining is done.

I dug up some synonyms for mining such as *quarry, excavate, dig (up), extract, unearth, remove, draw out and scoop out*. These synonyms connote the removal and shaking up of the normal, going beyond the surface layer, going beyond the norms, and going the extra mile. This suggests that some actions you would need to take will be discomforting for both you (the parent), and the child. You will need to sacrifice and invest yourself i.e., time, money, emotions, attitude, habits, desire, luxury, and much more. That is why parenting is not for the feeble minded; it is for those who are willing to be strong. Note that I did not say it is for the strong; it is not about your strength, but about your will to be strong for yourself and the children.

Parenting

Parenting refers to the intricacies of raising a child. It is not exclusive to a biological relationship. Parenting promotes and supports the physical, emotional, social, and intellectual development of a child from infancy to adulthood.

When I consider the word parenting, the biblical scripture that comes to heart, directing me on how to perform this duty is Psalms 127: 2-4:

In vain you rise early and stay up late, toiling for bread to eat—for He gives sleep to His beloved. Children are indeed a heritage from the LORD, and the fruit of the womb is His reward. Like arrows in the hand of a warrior, so are children born in one's youth...

I believe this scripture summarises how parents tend to strive to make ends meet for their children and family based on human understanding, while making several sacrifices in the process. Nevertheless, some of the sacrifices made in the process of the parents making ends meet come at the expense of the children themselves i.e. children may become emotionally neglected or miss out on parental affection and attention at the cost of parents' scale of preference.

Verse 2 reiterates how parents leave early for work and come back home late to provide for the family (not a bad thing in itself). Verse 3 talks about how children are gifts from God and why we have them. And verse 4 rounds it off with what children can represent to us their parents. The message translation emphasises how our enemies don't stand a chance against us when our quiver is full of well prepared (well-grounded) children.

So the question is what are you doing with these gifts of God– your child(ren)? Are you sacrificing for them or sacrificing them?

A prepared child is **ready, all set, equipped, primed, in a fit state, available, on hand, fixed, poised, and in position**, in their spirit, soul, and body.

A child like every other human being is a tripartite being that has spirit, soul, and body. As you equip them physically by providing shelter, food, and clothing, and intellectually by sending them to good schools, so you must deliberately equip their spirit and soul. Physical provision mostly caters for their body, while the school only caters to the intellectual part of their soul. I say this because, the soul consists of the mind (which includes the intellect), will, and emotions. So what most schools (especially in developing and underdeveloped countries) do is make provision to develop the intellect, which is still sometimes limited depending on the school's curriculum. So, what happens to other parts of the soul and the spirit? Who is equipping your child's emotions and willpower? Who or what is grooming their spirit too? Is it their friends, your maids, neighbours, electronic, social, or other type of media? This gives reason to why young and sometimes older adults have difficulty in making certain decisions or make a stance of their own. Some even lack personal beliefs, values, as well as social, adversity and emotional intelligence.

Your children are the arrows in your arms, yet they must take up arms themselves as they get older. They must be *armed*, trained, instructed, taught, educated, coached, tutored, groomed, disciplined, guided, directed, and made ready, strengthened, and fortified. How are you arming and fortifying your children for the future?

As parents you need to understand that there is a WAR where the lives of our children are concerned. The war is between the kingdom of light and darkness. Both kingdoms have agenda for children because they are the future. They are the ones that the Lord will use to continue to propagate His kingdom till His return. That is why verse 4 of Psalms 127 calls them arrows. They can either be receptive to the kingdom of God or darkness, depending on our preparation. You must get them into shape, get them set, and put them in the position to face the realities of life at the appropriate time. Doing this will help them to stand and take their place ready for the battle.

I repeat, THERE IS A WAR!

Truthfully, God has promised us victory in His word and has supplied us with more than we need for victory. He even says in 1 John 4:4 (NIV):

> *"You, dear children, are from God and have overcome them, because the one who is in you is greater than the one who is in the world."*

So, we certainly have victory by faith through Jesus Christ. He also promised to bless us (the fruit of our womb/loins and the produce of our land) in Deuteronomy 7:13:

> *"He will love you and bless you and multiply you. He will bless the fruit of your womb and the produce of your land--your grain, new wine, and oil--the young of your herds, and the new-born of your flocks, in the land that He swore to your fathers to give you."*

Nevertheless, as you do not fold your arms expecting your land to produce without you planting, so you must do your part by being faithful stewards in preparing these children for their excellent future. The farmer nurtures the plant by investing time, care, and constantly working the land. Likewise, you must invest love, quality time and hard work like you do to your careers and finances.

The word 'prepare' is a verb – that is a doing or action word. Most of the synonyms of 'prepare' listed above depict DOING, not just TALKING. As parents, we must show, we must Do, we must Walk the Talk, and not just Talk the Talk. The verb 'Do' is a deliberate action; it involves a person making a deliberate effort. To engage in this deliberate effort, we must be intentional about engaging our minds, which serve as reservoirs of what we know. We must start this work even before they are conceived and born. Why must we begin the work before they are born? To deliberately 'do' the work of preparing our children, there is a need to understand why we do what we do, and when it must be done.

As a trainer for Child Care Practice, the three foundational units we teach Levels 1 & 2 child care practitioners are 'Patterns of Child Development', 'Promoting Children's Development through Play', and 'The Principles of Early Years Practice'. The theory behind these three units suggests that there are certain things that adults should put in place for children's growth and development at specific age ranges for them to achieve their developmental milestones. The parents and caregivers of a child must put the necessary structure, boundaries, preparation, support, activities, effort amongst others for the child to be excellent at the right time. For every action, there is a purpose (conscious or unconscious), and for every purpose, there is a season.

Ecclesiastes 3:1-8 (Authorized King James Version) says

> *"To everything there is a season,*
> *and a time to every purpose under the heaven:*
> *² a time to be born, and a time to die;*
> *a time to plant, and a time to pluck up that which is planted;*
> *³ a time to kill, and a time to heal;*
> *a time to break down, and a time to build up;*
> *⁴ a time to weep, and a time to laugh;*
> *a time to mourn, and a time to dance;*
> *⁵ a time to cast away stones,*
> *and a time to gather stones together;*
> *a time to embrace, and a time to refrain from embracing;*
> *⁶ a time to get, and a time to lose;*
> *a time to keep, and a time to cast away;*
> *⁷ a time to rend, and a time to sew;*
> *a time to keep silence, and a time to speak;*

[8] *a time to love, and a time to hate;*
a time of war, and a time of peace."

Amplified Bible says, *"There is a season (a time appointed) for everything and a time for every delight and event or purpose under heaven"*. There is an appointed time to sow and to harvest. I like the way the Contemporary English Version says it *"Everything on earth has its own time and its own season"*.

There are things to be done from the womb and things to be done out of the womb. The next chapter will give insights on how your child's soul develops, and your role towards equipping not just their mind, but their will and emotions. It will provide more insights on why the foetal and early stage of children's life is paramount to how a child turns out later in life. It will also project the nitty-gritty involved in developing your child's soul by helping you understand how to take advantage and grasp the moments of the various seasons of your child's life, without living it to school and fate.

Your child's life is not included in the French saying *'que sera sera'* meaning what will be will be. Literally, you need to be intentional.

CHAPTER 2

"Development begins with large, uncontrolled (gross motor) movements before movements become precise and more refined"

— Arnold Gessell (1880-1961).

Understanding Child Psychology and Development

In the context of child growth and development, growth refers to the irreversible increase in size, while development refers to increase in skills and abilities. Both processes are highly dependent on genetic, nutritional, and environmental factors.

Although it is assumed that child development begins during infancy (when children are born), that is not the case. In child psychology, the prenatal period is considered an important part of the developmental process that sets the stage for future psychological development at the postnatal period. During this stage, the foetus goes through a remarkable change in size (length, weight, and head circumference), a reason why health professionals check these during ante-natal scans to ensure the baby's growth is proportionate. This is so they can monitor and intervene early enough if there is any growth or developmental issues with the foetus. As the child grows in the womb, the development of organs such as the brain also occurs; this continues developing throughout the course of the prenatal period and continues rapidly during the early years of childhood. The very-well-mind website summarises the process of prenatal development as occurring in three main stages namely: Germinal stage (first two weeks after conception), Embryonic stage (third to eighth week) and Foetal stage (ninth week till birth).

A pivotal stage of the child's prenatal period is the foetal[1] stage. The foetal stage is very critical to the wellbeing and development of a child because it is at this stage that the embryo becomes a foetus[2], and the brain begins to develop. During this stage, the brain and other organs that were already formed at the embryonic stage go through major changes and growth.

---

1 *fetal American English spelling.; foetal British English spelling*
2 *fetus American English spelling; foetus British English spelling*

Stages of Prenatal Development

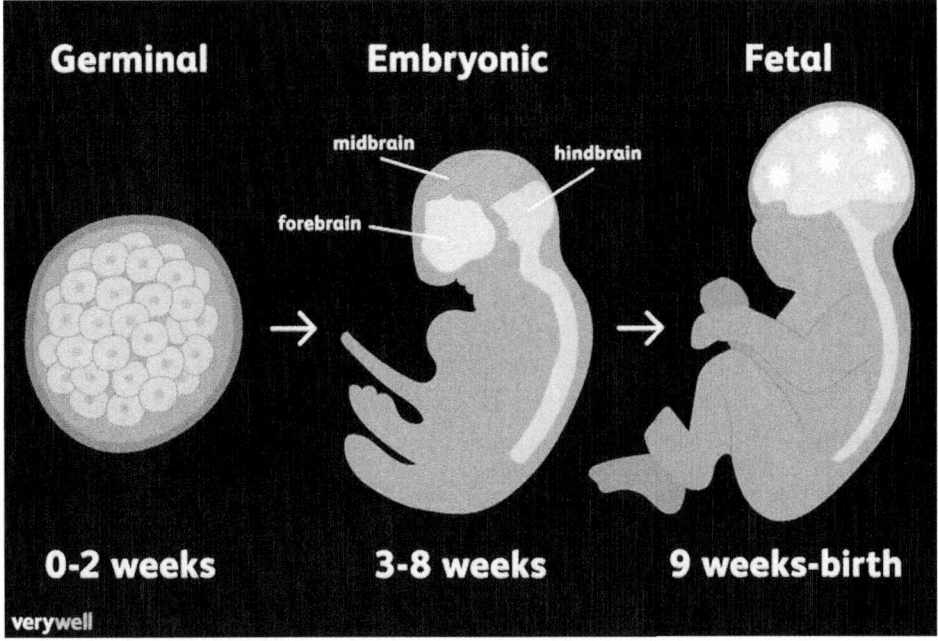

Figure 2.1 | verywellmind.com

Another important factor about this stage is that the brain and central nervous system begins to mature rapidly and become more responsive. Sensory perceptions and reflexes begin to emerge; the foetus begins to make reflexive motions with its arms and legs. This means that certain behavioural patterns begin to form as the child reacts to stimulus in the environment (both within and out of the womb).

Your Role

The little things we do while the foetus is in the womb could set the pace for the child's life development out of the womb. Foetal health issues can have detrimental effects on postnatal growth. Good pre-natal care is an essential factor in promoting foetal health and indirectly postnatal growth. Substances like alcohol, certain foods, as well as primary and secondary smoking is not recommended for pregnancy as they impact the brain development of the foetus. This is the stage when the mother should eat a healthy and balanced diet for the baby's brain development and to ensure a healthy and smart baby. For more information on foods to eat while pregnant, please see 'Baby Brain Development in Pregnancy: Stages & Foods to Eat' on parenting.firstcry.com.

Besides eating a healthy diet, parents can communicate with the foetus in words and in songs. It is also a good time to begin making your confessions of your heartfelt desires concerning the child. You can sing and speak words of affirmation to your child even while they are in the womb. I remember getting lots of jabs in response to my singing during my first pregnancy. Little wonder my girls have grown to love music so much. The things you do at this stage set the pace for their experience once they are outside the womb. Their learning does not start at home or at school, but while in the womb, where their recognition of words and sounds begins.

Be that as it may, brain development does not end at birth, but continues postnatal, growing in size and changing in structure. As children learn and experience the world, some areas of the brain are strengthened while other connections are pruned.

The first dynamic to children learning is through play. Play offers children a range of skills they will need when they start school so that they can understand their needs and other people's needs. In the Overview of Child Developmental Stages by California Department of Education, children's needs are characterised by the need for exploring and interaction. They need to be engaged actively, not by tablets, phones, screens, and other electronic devices, rather through interactions and play that can shape their mind, will and emotions, as well as promote the inquisitiveness for more.

The interaction that a child has with their parent or caregivers helps them to process language, cognitive and social skills which form the foundations for social interaction in the child's brain. If a child does not receive enough interaction in the early developmental stages, it can have negative implications for their communication in the future. This is a fact I have seen evolve in myself and in some other children around me.

A book titled *The Absorbent Mind* written by one of the greatest educators ever, Maria Montessori explains how a child's mind has a sponge-like capacity. It describes a child's mind as having the sponge-like capacity to absorb everything necessary to create an individual, including language and culture. She postulates that the absorbent period of a child is approximately from the first 6 years of life, where the child absorbs everything from their environment. This implies that children, especially in the early years are like little sponges, soaking up and absorbing countless amount of information around them, effortlessly, continuously, and indiscriminately.

The brain of a young child is sponge-like such that they can develop approximately 90% of their core brain structure by the time they are five years old. Learning comes naturally to babies and young children. As they grow physically day by day, they are also soaking up experiences emotionally, socially, and mentally, whilst developing their intelligence and understanding of the world around them. Their mind works differently from that of adults. The things that a young child sees are not just remembered; they form part of their soul.

Montessori also divided the 'absorbent mind' phase into two stages: the unconscious and conscious stages, to suggest that children, like little sponges, involuntarily absorb information around them, then gradually make sense of it actively.

At the unconscious stage (from birth to age three), the child absorbs information unconsciously or unknowingly. They develop basic functions i.e., sit, stand, walk, use their hands, speak, etc., without conscious effort on their part, through imitation. If you observe your toddler, you will notice them imitating what they see, gradually developing towards their next stage of development. The most important time in a child's life is their first 1000 days i.e. from birth to age three; their brains are developing faster than at any other time.

The conscious stage is from ages three to about six years old. The child at this stage still has a sponge-like mind that absorbs information easily but is **now** intentionally seeking specific information as they expand newly developed faculties and abilities. At this stage the child is predisposed toward learning things like order, sequencing, early math, music, and letter shapes/sounds which are the building blocks for the math, reading, and writing skills to come. If you observe children this age, you will notice them demonstrating an intense desire to make personal choices to accomplish tasks independently.

The parent or care giver is the child's first teacher; they play a vital role in helping young children learn through play and activities. Hence, as a parent, interact with your babies and young children. Do not leave the interaction to other media such as toys and screens. I am repeating this because it is the easiest thing to do. Have you noticed that it is easier to do something for a child than to talk them through how to do it? Yes, I know the feeling. However if you do it yourself, the youngster will not benefit as much as they would if you demonstrated and explained how to do it. That is what interaction is about, and young children excel in learning and understanding this way through interactive play.

In the next section of this chapter, I would like to lay a background on the psychological dynamism of the seasons to be mindful of in parenting for excellence, especially with regards to the soul. This will be done with reference to the stages of life where I will be using a theory of one of the great child development psychologists, Erik Erikson. It's important to note that because it is a theory, it can be critiqued. One of its criticisms is that it does not provide the exact mechanisms and details about how an individual can move from one stage to the next. However, understanding these stages can be helpful to understand how to prepare, equip and instruct your child at different phases of their life, particularly childhood.

CHAPTER 3

Seasons to be Mindful for in Parenting for Excellence

A remarkable child psychologist, Erik Erikson proposed the theory of the Psychosocial Development concerned with people becoming competent in each stage of life. Erikson was interested in how social interaction and relationships affect development and growth. Unlike many other developmental theories, Erikson's theory addresses changes that occur across the entire lifespan, from birth to death. He noted that people progress through a series of stages as they grow and change throughout life. This also explains another principle of child development – that development is sequential. Each stage of childhood development lays a precept and paves way for the next stage of development. This means that each stage builds on the preceding stage.

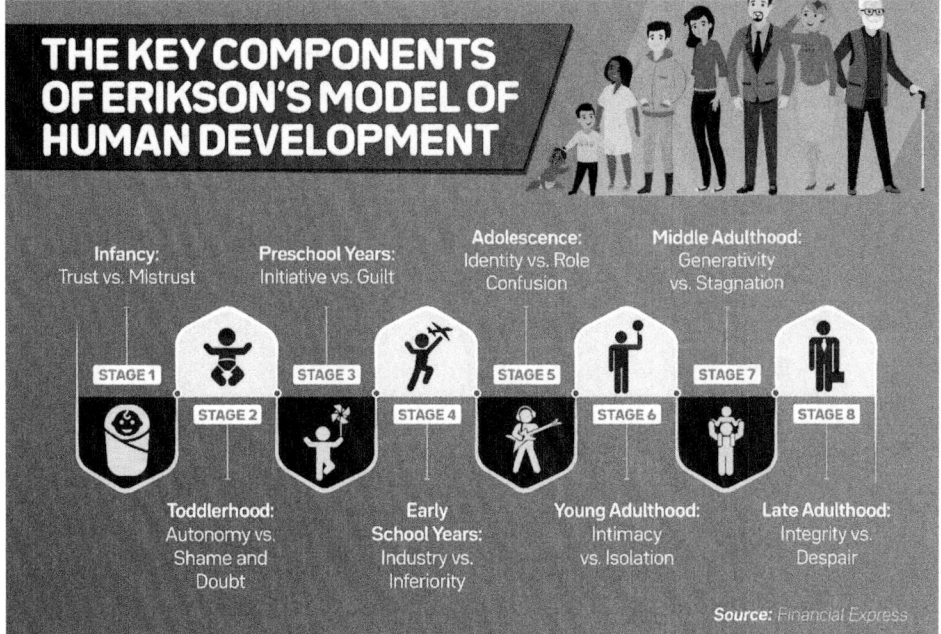

Figure3.1

This is why one of the principles of child development states that development is holistic, implying that the five areas of development are linked and connected. When a child begins to move around (physical development), their movement paves way for them to explore their environment, acquire new concepts they could put into memory, as well as develop their creativity and imagination (cognitive development). Furthermore, children begin to communicate through gestures or words based on their information processing which is then the foundation for making emotional connections and interacting socially with people around them.

The Key Ares of Development

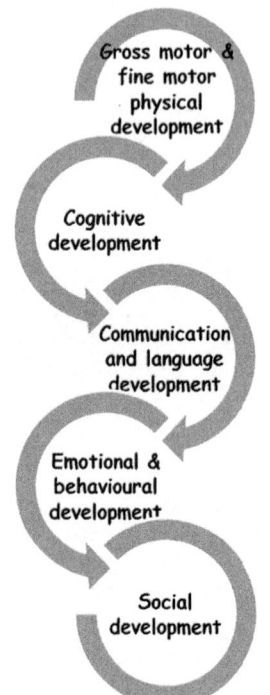

Figure 3.2

Being a psychosocial theory, the theory does not focus on the obvious physical changes that occur as children grow up, but rather on the socio-emotional factors that influence an individual's psychological growth. The theory postulates that at the boundary of each stage of development, everyone experiences certain developmental 'conflict' centred on the ability or inability to 'develop psychological quality.' In other words, these conflicts must be resolved in order to successfully develop the significant virtue of that stage. Children and adults are therefore faced with mastering the developmental task primarily to that stage.

Erikson affirms that when an individual is able to successfully overcome the conflicts in each stage, they emerge with some competence or psychosocial strength that will serve them for the rest of their lives. Their long-term wellbeing is enhanced by this. Whereas failure to deal with these conflicts effectively could impact the individual's ability to develop the skills needed to develop a strong sense of self-esteem and self-concept. This is because the individual feels a sense of mastery, ego, or competence when they can successfully deal with each stage which then determines their mindset (self-concept, self-image, and self-esteem), as well as their behaviour and actions. But in the absence of this, the individual could develop a sense of inadequacy or weakness in that area of development or subsequent life stages.

For instance, for the first stage of human development, trust is the primary conflict. Being able to trust is an ability that contributes to emotional health throughout life during both childhood and adulthood. Failing to master these critical conflicts could result in social and emotional struggles that last a lifetime.

Erikson's Psychosocial Stages: A Summary Chart

Age	Conflict	Important Events	Outcome
Infancy (birth to 18 months)	Trust vs. Mistrust	Feeding	Hope
Early Childhood (2 to 3 years)	Autonomy vs. Shame and Doubt	Toilet Training	Will
Preschool (3 to 5 years)	Initiative vs. Guilt	Exploration	Purpose
School Age (6 to 11 years)	Industry vs. Inferiority	School	Confidence
Adolescence (12 to 18 years)	Identity vs. Role Confusion	Social Relationships	Fidelity
Young Adulthood (19 to 40 years)	Intimacy vs. Isolation	Relationships	Love
Middle Adulthood (40 to 65 years)	Generativity vs. Stagnation	Work and Parenthood	Care
Maturity (65 to death)	Ego Integrity vs. Despair	Reflection on Life	Wisdom

Table 3.1

Erikson's psychosocial stages of the human life summarised on Table3.1 highlights the eight stages of human life represented in Figure 3.1, as well as the conflicts, important events, and desired outcomes. In order to understand how to deliberately prepare your child for an excellent future at these stages, there is then a need to further understand how children master these crisis or conflicts for the desired outcome. There is also the need to discuss the roles of parents or primary care givers in this respect. The following discussion will be subject to the first four stages of life, which are infancy, early childhood, preschool, and school age since these stages are critical to how the child turns out and succeeds in the later stages in life. This conclusion is also based on our definitions of the child stated in Chapter 1; hence the need for awareness on how to maximise this period.

Stage 1: Infancy (Trust vs. Mistrust)

This stage begins at birth and lasts until your child is around 18 months old. It is the fundamental and most important stage in a child's life out of the womb. It shapes their view of the world and their overall personality. This is the stage where children undergo their first psychosocial conflict; emerging with the reasoning "Can I trust the people around me?"

Ideally, infants are almost entirely dependent on their caregivers who are mostly their parents. They depend on them for everything they need to survive including food, love, warmth, safety, and nurturing. Hence, developing trust is based on the dependability and quality of the child's parents. So, it is no surprise that how parents interact with their babies has a profound effect on both their physical and mental health. If a parent fails to provide adequate love and care, the child will come to feel that they cannot trust or depend on the adults in their life.

Early patterns of trust help children build a strong base of trust that's crucial for their social and emotional development (will and emotions). If a child successfully develops trust, they will feel safe and secure in the world. You as the caregiver are essentially shaping their personality and determining how they will view the world. In other words, the child's overall perception of the world and trust is dependent on how the child is introduced to the world.

Moreover, children who learn to trust their caregivers in infancy will be more likely to form trusting relationships with others throughout the course of their lives. Trust at this stage includes believing in the caregivers (parents), trusting that the world is safe, and knowing that their needs will be met. The opposite of this would mean the child distrusting caregivers, fearing the world, and being unsure that their needs will be met. A child's ability to trust helps them develop a strong self-image, esteem, and competence, functional for forming healthy attachments during childhood and adulthood.

Since this stage serves as a foundation of development that can influence the rest of an individual's life, it is essential for parents to provide responsive, dependable care.

Your Role

Early experiences of nurturing, feeding and care are rich sources of new learning. The rapport that develops between parent and child at this stage becomes a bond that is fundamental to social learning and the child's sense of security and wellbeing.

The primary way to build trust with your baby is to respond when they try to communicate with you bearing in mind that they cannot use words to express themselves. A significant way that babies communicate what they are feeling is through crying, and it carries different meanings. Usually, babies cry to let you know that they need one of the following:

- Affection
- Comfort
- Food

It is important for parents and caregivers to provide comfort to an infant by holding them close and securely. This provides both warmth and physical contact. Feeding, bathing, and comforting your child helps them learn to trust that their needs will be met.

Every baby communicates differently, so becoming familiar with your baby's communication style is a key to success at this stage. It is said that noticing and responding to these signals, whether they are cries, body movements, coos, or even words, helps them learn to trust you and the world around them. I remember thinking once I have fed the baby and the baby is safe, there is no further need to keep holding the baby close to avoid getting the child too attached and utterly used to being carried all the time. Even though it is ideal to gradually support a child to become less independent on their major caregiver, I did not know I was depriving the young child of her right to comfort and affection. I was detaching myself at the wrong stage of her life. Actions like this could backfire and make the child feel insecure when they do not get enough attention from you at this stage. Some children may develop a pattern or habit of being naughty if they get attention only when they are mischievous. But when the child knows that "I can always go to mum or dad for a quick hug or show of affection", they will not see the need to throw a tantrum before they get attention. Selah!

It is also worthy to note here that building this trust does not just imply what you do for the child, but what you do with them. One major action you can do with your baby to meet their needs at this stage is playing with them. I might seem to be overemphasising this, but play cannot be overemphasised. Play is as important for the child in the womb as it is outside the womb. Play is one of the main ways in which children learn. It helps to build self-worth by giving a child a sense of his or her own abilities and to feel good about themselves. Because it's fun, children often become very absorbed in what they are doing, which helps them develop the ability to concentrate.

Children learn through all their senses – tasting, touching, seeing, hearing, and smelling. By watching and copying people close to them, they also learn language and behaviour. When you play with them or do anything close to them, they copy you.

An example of play that you can engage your child with during their first three months is what is commonly known as "tummy time." Tummy Time is supervised playtime that babies spend on their stomachs while awake. It helps to strengthen the bones in the neck, back and arms. This type of play also lays the foundation for getting the child ready for independence, higher-level fine motor skills, as well as speech and feeding skills that should come later.

Other examples of play activities you can engage them with at this stage include rolling on the floor together, smiling at and with them, shaking rattles, clapping, singing, making facial expressions and sounds that they can possibly copy and recognise later, sitting with them and modelling toy use, talking and listening to them, tidying up toys together from when they are about 12 months old. These activities will help the child to develop their physical, cognitive, emotional, social, language and communication skills, whilst their view of the world is being enhanced. Talking and singing to them from their first day in the world (as well as in the womb) helps to develop their memory of sounds and later, words.

Also, it is proven that reading to your child as babies will ignite their reading habit and eventually support their language acquisition for other areas of development. Little wonder why available and deliberate parents are referred to as their child's first teacher.

Similarly, providing children with a variety of safe and interesting objects they can touch and explore will help learning in several ways. For example, a basket of everyday materials that won't cause any harm to them such as: wooden spoons, wooden bowls, plastic plates, wooden or fabric blocks, silk scarves, rubber sponge, metal cups, small toys with bells, socks, and other household materials that they cannot choke on. This type of basket is referred to as a 'treasure basket' because it contains multidimensional treasures that babies can touch and explore to simultaneously advance the child's five areas of development. Through touching, exploring, and looking at shapes and textures of objects, they feed their curiosity and develop their ability to distinguish different shapes, textures, and colours. Later in life, this helps them learn to do things, such as reading, when they identify the different shapes of letters.

Ultimately, children raised by consistently unreliable, unpredictable parents who fail to meet these basic needs eventually develop an overall sense of mistrust. Mistrust can cause children to become fearful, confused, and anxious, all of which make it difficult to form healthy relationships. This, in turn, can lead to poor social- loneliness, emotional-isolation, and adversity-giving up easily quotients later in life, if not well handled.

No child is going to develop a sense of 100% trust or 100% doubt. Successful development is all about striking a balance between trust and mistrust. When this happens, children acquire hope, which Erikson described as 'openness to experience tempered by some wariness that danger might be present.' So, decide on a couple of things you will start doing with your baby from today to improve their chances of excellence at this stage.

Stage 2: Early Childhood (Autonomy vs. Shame and Doubt)

This occurs from about 18 months to age 3 with focus on developing a greater sense of personal control. Children at this stage are mostly referred to as toddlers. This stage builds upon the earlier stage and serves as an important building block for the stages to come. During the previous stage of development, children were entirely dependent on others for their care and safety; the foundation for trust was built. However, as they progress into the second stage, it becomes important for young children to begin to develop a sense of personal independence and control. As they learn to do things for themselves, they establish a sense of control over themselves as well as some basic confidence in their own abilities.

Children at this age become increasingly independent and want to gain more control over what they do and how they do it. They start to gain some independence by performing basic actions such as toilet training, on their own. Toilet training plays a major role as learning to control one's body functions leads to a feeling of control and a sense of independence.

Other important events at this stage of development include more control and decision making over food choices, toy preferences, and clothing selection. The child often feels the need to do things independently, e.g., picking out what they will wear each day, putting on their own clothes, and deciding what they will eat. Although this can often be frustrating for parents, it is an important part of developing a sense of self-control and personal autonomy.

Parents need to seek a balance for their children at this stage as much as possible. Erikson believed that achieving a balance between autonomy and shame/doubt would lead to will. 'Will' in this context is the belief that children can act intentionally, within reason and limits. Children who are successful at this stage would be able to develop the virtue of 'will', that is self-reliance, otherwise known as a 'can-do attitude'. They will feel secure and confident, while those who do not are left with a sense of inadequacy, shame, and self-doubt. Consequently, children who are on the path of mastery and have confidence in their skills are more likely to succeed in subsequent tasks and gain mastery of their spirit, soul, and body.

Your Role

One of the characteristics of children's development is that children develop at different rates and will reach milestones at a rate that is unique to them. For instance, my first daughter took her first steps just before she turned 10 months but had only two teeth when she turned one, whereas my second daughter took her first steps at about 13 months and had six teeth by the time she turned one. Being able to walk earlier or having more teeth at age one does not determine the smartness of either child, it just means one might be able to move around more easily and probably explore more because of mobility, than the other, while the other's babbling and range of eating could be more diverse at that particular age. Eventually, they may still be able to do about the same thing at 18 months, except there is a medical condition or disability that hinders it.

This is just a gentle reminder that children will get to each developmental stage when they are ready; the more reason why caregivers, particularly parents, should not compare a child with another. You should accept that each child grows and develops at his or her own pace. Avoid comparisons with other children and try not to put a child under pressure to do anything she or he is not ready to do. This applies equally to walking, potty training, reading, and writing. Nevertheless, there are things that adults can do to lovingly support the child to facilitate their development. For instance, to encourage reading from an early age, you can be proactive with actions such as reading and talking about the pictures in books with your child. You can also support the child for bigger physical movements like running, jumping, throwing, by watching for their cues that they are ready to advance, celebrating every achievement, giving help when needed, comforting a fall, encouraging your baby to walk to you as you extend your hands toward them, etc. If the child has mastered walking on flat surfaces, you could also challenge them to walking up and down a ramp or ask them to follow you.

Like you and I, a child can do anything within their milestones or even more, if they are nurtured in the right environment and with the right elements like praise, kindness, love, care, and positivity. I will talk more about nurturing children's ability to stretch and absorb in Chapter 5.

A major area that children attain autonomy is in toilet training, i.e., being able to know when to use the potty or toilet without any prompt. Since potty training is essential to children developing a sense of independence, children who struggle with potty training and who are shamed for their urine or bowel accidents (wetting themselves) are likely to lack a sense of personal control, hence the feeling of shame and doubt. For this reason, parents will need to support the child towards attaining independence with regards to developing personal control over toileting.

Your role to seek balance in this aspect is to endeavour that you handle any 'accident' as positively as possible; that you support the child to understand that having accidents does not make the child a failure. It would mean that you support the child to continue to have the will to keep trying rather than give up. These strive for balance must be evident not just in your words but also in your non-verbal reactions or actions. This could mean not shouting at the child because of their accidents, praising or rewarding toileting achievements, being sensitive of the situation, not comparing the child with another who has attained autonomy, as well as seeking right counsel or advice.

For some ideas on how to support your child for autonomy in this area, you can check out *Emma Hubbard's YouTube video on The Truth About Potty Training (6 Mistakes You Need to Avoid)*. I found this useful when I felt my younger daughter's potty training was taking too long because of 'too many accidents' she was having. Some of the ideas I got from the video which I would recommend to any parent struggling with this is to avoid punishing or yelling at the child for accidents. Avoid letting the child sit on a potty beyond 5 minutes at a time. I found the latter very interesting because my daughter had begun to dread the potty. She saw it as a form of punishment or as a deterrent to keep her from moving around freely because I would say to her "you're not getting up until you've done a wee in the potty."

Parents can also help children develop a sense of autonomy by allowing them make choices and to gain a sense of independence. This is called child empowerment in the Early Years Foundation Stage (EYFS) statutory framework. Empowering children helps children develop self-confidence which they will find useful as they grow older in all spheres of life. It is not unusual for children to first make large uncontrolled decisions, but it is our place as parents to guide them until they make precise and more refined decisions in life. Some ways to empower the child for independence and decision making at this stage is by providing a variety of positive choices e.g. for clothing and toys, you can provide two options of clothing you would like them to wear, or toys you would like them to play with, from which they can choose.

Try to avoid doing everything for the child. As they develop, let them experiment and work things out for themselves, even if it means that they make mistakes sometimes, e.g. putting clothes on the wrong way. This helps them develop independence and confidence in their abilities. When you empower a toddler to do things for themselves. It also shows that you trust them, and that they should believe in that trust.

Another area that this sense of autonomy vs shame and doubt comes to play is in a child's ability to feed themselves without spilling or making too much mess. As the adult, how you react to your child making a mess or spilling things will determine if a child has the will to persist and act intentionally within reason and limits.

I recently learned that a child can also gain autonomy with meal choices as long as it is within reason and limits. Traditionally, parents would dish the food into the child's plate without necessarily telling them why that is the chosen meal or the benefit of the meal to their body. I understand some families have limited choices due to financial limitation, however, even the little or limited choice can still be used as a tool of communication. You can talk to the child about the food option, the taste, its benefit, as well as the benefits of making the right choices. For instance, you could explain why taking water instead of fizzy or carbonated drinks is healthier. It is also an avenue for young children to learn the classes of food and their benefits.

Do not just put food in their plates, rather provide a selection of nutritious food that you can afford. You can lay them out on the dining table or on your child's table if eating separately, and then they pick what they want to eat into their plate. For example, if what you have is beans, or bread, lay it out on the table (with some veggies if possible) and encourage them to dish their own food themselves. Of course, I did not grow up selecting whatever I wanted; this is what I gleaned from Erikson's theory and training sessions for preparing my child for pre-school at age four. This is also a means to preparing them for school and the outside world. Being able to select and stick to their own meal during break time in school does not just give them a sense of autonomy and making the right choices, it is also an early way for them to begin practising decisiveness and sticking with their decisions (stick-to-itiveness); a skill that even some adults lack.

For parents that are worried that their children will begin to make unnecessary demands, remember the child is choosing from a selection of options that they can see laid out on the table; not food that is not available in your home or that only exists on TV or in their imagination. Practising this with your child also teaches your child contentment, even when you are not with them. Certain things will not really matter or be a big deal to them because their 'will' i.e., decisiveness has already been ignited from a tender age. Also, this skill of autonomy would prevent your child from easily falling for peer pressure when they are older and save you from unnecessary stress too.

Stage 3: Preschool (Initiative vs. Guilt)

The third stage of psychosocial development takes place during the preschool years, which is between ages 3 to 5. This is a more conscious stage of development. The major theme of this stage of psychosocial development is that children begin to assert control and power over the environment through play and other social interactions. During this time, children begin to learn that they can exert power over themselves and the world. They begin to consciously control their world in small ways by exploring, seeking specific information, and trying new things. However, trying new things poses the risk of failure. Success at this stage relies on a healthy balance between initiative and guilt.

Initiative in this context refers to the enthusiastic desire to attempt new tasks, join or come up with activities with friends, and use new skills in play. Initiative leads to a sense of purpose and can help develop leadership skills. Children who develop initiative acquire a sense of purpose and feel capable and able to lead others. They are eager to try new activities and experiences without excessive fear of failure. They learn what they can and cannot control. When they make mistakes, they don't feel guilty; they understand that they just need to try again. Trying things on their own and exploring their own abilities can help them develop ambition and direction.

On the other hand, children who don't develop initiative at this stage are left with a sense of guilt and self-doubt. Guilt refers to shame resulting from failing to complete a task successfully, and/or feeling embarrassed over attempting something. Children who experience guilt interpret mistakes as a sign of personal failure or weakness and feel that they are somehow "bad."

A child who feels more guilt than initiative at this stage may begin to resist trying new things for fear of failing. When they make efforts toward something, they may feel that they are doing something wrong, almost as if they are inadequate or lack self-efficacy. I understand this could sometimes provoke irritation in adults, but adults need to also understand children better. Guilt emerges and initiative diminishes when the child is not taught resilience and persistence in the face of difficulty, but success at this stage will produce a child who, after failing a task, keeps trying, rather than giving up; hence the child having a sense of purpose.

Your Role

Your primary role at this stage is to teach the child resilience and persistence.

Children need to begin asserting control and power by taking initiative. This could involve children planning activities, accomplishing tasks, and facing challenges. They should begin to understand that things would not necessarily go the way they expect and pick themselves up regardless.

At this stage, one of the ways children develop initiative, resilience and persistence is through play and imagination. It is important for caregivers, particularly parents, to give children the freedom and space to learn and explore their world through their play, as well as encourage them to make appropriate choices. When caregivers stifle children's efforts to engage in physical and imaginative play, children begin to feel that their self-initiated efforts are a source of embarrassment.

I have worked in an 'international school' where children barely had the opportunity to go out to play during break due to syllabus overload. There was always so much work to do in the classroom that all the students did during break was to take 10 minutes to eat their lunch in the classroom hastily, then get back to work. I always queried the fact that the children did not have enough opportunity to burn energy and explore their environment through play which is another form of learning. Some toddlers at preschools even rarely sing rhymes and barely engage in any imaginative play. Some pre-school classrooms do not even have imaginative play areas like dress-up corner. I have also seen parents who do not allow children to move freely in their living area (sitting room) at home, or they always box away toys too often because they don't want an untidy space.

Think about it, if your child is going to such schools mentioned earlier, where there is no opportunity to explore, imagine, initiate activities and be creative, and you also don't provide these opportunities at home, what do you think is happening to the child's soul (will, mind, and emotions)? Do you think learning how to write alphabets and numbers, as well as screen time, are all the child needs to be equipped at this stage? Certainly not! There is so much more to getting a child ready for school beyond helping with words and numbers. Children also learn through play and interactions. Play offers children a range of skills they will need when they start school so that they can understand theirs' and other people's needs. You can help them by providing a range of play ideas and objects to aid their school readiness for their next stage. We can do better! You can do better!

On another note, the solution to having a tidy space is not hindering play. As a mindful parent, do not seek to have a perfect space or living area at the detriment of your child's development. I am not saying your space should be like a dump; that won't help the child psychologically either. Rather, you could create a space or section in your living room as your children's play area if you cannot afford to have a second living room. In any case, you might need to child-proof the space to ensure the child(ren)'s safety while playing and exploring. You would also need to encourage the child(ren) to tidy up after play. Of course, this would mean you model the exercise of tidying up to them by doing it with them a few times until they get into the habit themselves.

I remember when we lived in a two-bedroom flat in Ilupeju, Lagos. We had a children's corner in a section of our living room where the girls could play with their toys and explore as much as possible to their delight, while being within the reach of any adult in case of any emergency. This was to ensure the girls could play, learn, and have fun without turning the space upside down. At times they would still bring their toys and play towards the main living area, but at the end of play, we encouraged them to return their toys or tidy up.

Sometimes, I would join them in their corner and join the play. I would pretend to be their patient (human or animal) while the child is a human or vet doctor, and the other child, the assistant or nurse. Play with your children as it is an opportunity to show your interest and delight in their discoveries and achievements. Now they are older, we play ludo and board games - I occasionally let them win by not playing competitively and at other times, I decide to play competitively where I win hands down. I use this as an opportunity to teach them resilience and persistence (to keep trying regardless of the situation). It is also a good time to chat with them and know what's going on in their spirit, soul, and body. One of the best ways to help children feel valued is to listen to them and let them know when they are doing something well.

This practice of exploring the environment without too many restrictions helps the child feel excited about exercising some control over what they're doing, hence resilience and persistence. Parents who are discouraging or dismissive may cause children to feel ashamed of themselves and to become overly dependent upon the help of others. Try to give toddlers and young children space to enjoy physical movement and games. This includes running, skipping, climbing, playing ball games in parks and playgrounds or your garden. Use creative play to help them develop their abilities and skills. Another important benefit of freedom of play is that the child is also developing their imaginative and creative aspects of cognitive development.

Another aspect to look out for is how adults react when children make mistakes. I remember growing up, beating myself up every time I made mistakes; I did this so much I barely had the desire to try out new things. Even as an adult, I used to feel uncomfortable giving an opinion on a subject for fear of failure. Interestingly, I began to observe a similar sense of guilt in my 8-year-old daughter. Her teacher -thanks to her- also reported similar observations. After conversing with my daughter, I realised that I had often pushed for perfection so much that we were losing hold of balance; thankfully it could be mitigated. To help prevent feelings of guilt, and to teach persistence and resilience, parents can encourage children to see their mistakes as learning opportunities. That's how we adopted the motto 'mistakes are for learning'. It's very important that adults avoid excessive criticism, ridicule, and dismissiveness at this stage. Instead, they should encourage children to keep trying through practice and persistence.

A good way to encourage this is by modelling it to your child. If you make mistakes, own it, apologise (where necessary) and move on by verbalising the decision to try again. Encouraging a child's natural curiosity without judgment or impatience is very important. Yes, you've got to be patient with your reactions regardless of your state of mind. Furthermore, acknowledge and reinforce every positive step towards accomplishing tasks, and facing challenges. Try to let them know when they are doing things well and at other times, aim for a firm but gentle approach. This does not diminish the fact that children still need to be shown clear boundaries i.e., to be told and shown what behaviour is and is not acceptable and why, as they develop. Parents mostly stop at the non-acceptable behaviour without providing a reason. Children are naturally curious and will always want to know about 'cause and effect' of actions. This also forms part of their learning and preparation for years to come. If possible, try to ensure that other adults that help you care for your child can use this approach too whilst providing a stimulating environment for your child.

I must say that plying this route might be daunting or even frustrating for parents and other care givers as children begin exercising more control over who to play with, the activities they engage in, and the way that they approach different tasks. For instance, parents and other adults might want to guide children toward certain choices, but children might resist and insist on making their own choices. This might sometimes lead to conflict; however, it is important to give children the chance to make their own choices within safe boundaries. This is because children who are over-directed by adults are likely to struggle to develop a sense of initiative and confidence in their own abilities. Be guided by the child and observe what s/he is able to do and encourage them gradually to build on what they are able to do.

Overall, the key to supporting the child at this stage is to continue to enforce safe boundaries and encourage them to make good choices using modelling and reinforcement.

Stage 4: School age (Industry vs. Inferiority)

One of the major objectives of EYFS framework is for children within the early childhood stage (2 to 5 years) to learn to play with other children co-operatively. They encourage this by providing play opportunities that promote turn taking such as painting a mural, putting a puzzle together, pretend-play recreating everyday life scenarios (e.g. playing grocery store, doctor's office, or veterinarian), blowing bubbles, using slides or swings, and constructing using building blocks. This allows children to work together towards a common goal instead of in opposition to one another or in pursuit of winning. This social expertise begins to get more popular when the children attain the age of 4 to 5 years.

The interactive skills acquired at the preschool phase play an important role during the fourth psychosocial stage which takes place during the primary school years from approximately ages 6 to 12. This is the Industry versus Inferiority stage. A child's social world expands considerably as they enter school and gain new friendships with peers. Unlike the earlier stages, where a child's interactions were centred primarily on caregivers, family members, and others in their immediate household, as the school years begin, the realm of social influence increases dramatically, and through social interactions, children begin to develop a sense of pride in their accomplishments and abilities.

The first three stages set the foundation for this stage, notwithstanding, this is the very critical stage for the child. This is the stage when the school (teachers and peers) and more so parents' encouragement and support matter most. Events at this stage can build or undermine self-confidence. The positive or negative experiences of their early childhood could either develop for better or for worse at this stage.

This is also when learning expectations progress from the usual play and exploration. At earlier stages of development, children were mostly able to engage in activities for fun, as well as receive praise and attention. But once real school begins, actual performance and skills are evaluated. At this point, learning becomes more demanding and academic. Grades and feedback from educators encourage kids to pay more attention to the actual quality of their work. Children are recognised and may be rewarded for performing various tasks such as reading, writing, drawing, and solving problems during school and other social activities. Kids who do well in school are more likely to develop a sense of competence and confidence. They feel good about themselves and their ability to succeed.

It is also the stage where some parents are likely to be unavailable because they are trying to earn additional income to cater for the increasing demands of life i.e., paying for tuition, holidays, and general upkeep. However, children need the availability and encouragement of their parents, as well as the commendations of teachers to cope with these new academic and social demands. Children who are motivated and complimented by parents and teachers develop a feeling of competence and belief in their skills and abilities to handle tasks set before them. Those who receive little or no encouragement from parents, teachers, or peers will doubt their ability to be successful. Hence, success at this phase leads to a sense of competence, while failure results in feelings of inferiority.

Consequently, as noted with earlier stages, children who don't feel competent in their ability to succeed may be less likely to try new things and more likely to assume that their efforts will not measure up under scrutiny. During the school years, children who struggle with schoolwork may have a harder time developing these feelings of competence, and may be left with feelings of failure, inadequacy, and inferiority. And this could set the stage for later problems in development.

Your Role

Proficiency at play and schoolwork helps children to develop a sense of competence and pride in their abilities. By feeling competent and capable, children can also form a strong sense of self-concept and self-confidence.

During social interactions with peers, some children may discover that they have more abilities than their peers in certain aspects. This can lead to feelings of confidence. In other cases, children may discover that they are not quite as capable as the other kids, which can result in feelings of inadequacy. To foster success during this stage, it is important for both parents and teachers to offer support and inspiration. Even if children struggle in some areas of school, encouraging children in areas in which they excel can help foster feelings of competence and achievement. However, adults should be careful not to equate achievement with acceptance and love. Unconditional love and support from adults can help all children through this stage, particularly those who may struggle with feelings of inferiority.

On the other hand, children who are overly praised might develop a sense of arrogance. Parents can help children develop a sense of realistic competence by avoiding excessive praise and rewards, encouraging efforts rather than outcome, and helping kids develop a growth mindset. A growth mindset is where the individual believes 'I'm an evolving work in progress, I can learn to do anything I want, I only fail when I stop trying, mistakes are for learning'. This is a much better place to be rather than having a fixed mindset that says 'That's just who I am. I can't change it, either I'm good at it or I'm not, what will be will be, if I don't try, then I won't fail.' Clearly, balance plays a major role at this stage of development.

To further consolidate your understanding of your role in equipping your child at this stage, it might be worthwhile using a case study to discuss. In teaching BTEC, we use a lot of case studies to help learners fully grasp concepts being taught.

Case Study

There are two children 'Zach and Jane' both in Year 5 (ages 9-10) in the same primary school. Zach does well in English and Arts but finds science lessons difficult. His parents are willing to and make time to help him each evening with his homework. He also asks the teacher for help and starts to receive affirmation for his efforts and the teacher also boosts his morale.

Jane is good with some subjects but also struggles with science, and her parents do not seem to be available or interested in assisting her with her homework. They got her a teacher to help at home once a week, but she doesn't feel it is helping much. She feels bad about the poor grades she receives in her science assignments but is not sure what to do about the situation. Her schoolteacher is critical of Jane's work but does not offer her any extra assistance or advice. Eventually, Jane just gives up, and her grades become even worse.

While both children struggle with this aspect of school, Zach receives the support and encouragement he needs to overcome these difficulties and still build a sense of mastery. However, Jane lacks the social and emotional encouragement she needs. Who do you think is likely to develop a sense of industry, and who will be left with feelings of inferiority?

This affirms that schools alone cannot help to prepare and equip the totality of a child (especially the soul). Truthfully, as a teacher, I understand the pressure that teachers face daily with workload. I know the grass is not greener anywhere else, but it is hard to find teachers who just keep giving and giving themselves unconditionally to the child, as parents should or would.

Parents, you need to make the right provision and set things in place properly and deliberately to mine excellence out of your child's will, mind, intellect, and emotions. You should devote more time to creating an enabling environment at this stage. Make it easier for your child(ren) to talk to you. Understand that the work you have put in place in the earlier stages will be put to test at this stage. Likewise, the adolescent stage (13-17years) will be testing all that has been mined at the entire childhood stage (0-12 years). That is when it seems like they are pulling away from you.

Reflect on what you are presently doing to equip your child at whatever stage they are and consider what you can now do better.

CHAPTER 4

Your Child's Spirit

"Excellence comes from within."

— **Author Unknown**

The child is a spirit that has a soul and lives in a body just like adults. Parenting does not end with providing children good food, clothing, shelter, and academic education. Preparing, training, equipping, instructing, and grooming the child goes beyond their intellectual and personal development. Excellence is not just about academics or morals but a total package (Spirit, Soul, and Body). Parents enrol children in extracurricular activities and clubs like karate, piano, etc. to work towards developing the child's mind, intellect, and physical skills, but neglect the most important part of their being which is the spirit.

Guy Finley says, "knowledge without spirit is like finding yourself on a cold night with all the wood in the world and no flame to ignite it". This suggests that knowledge without a kindled spirit is as good as death. No matter the knowledge amassed, if a person's spirit is not fired up, it will all be redundant or pointless. That is why the first thing the devil attacks is the spirit before anything else. Once the spirit is weak, every other component of the person is done for. Therefore it is necessary to train, prepare and equip your child spiritually.

The question then is "What and how do you feed your children spiritually? Do they see you pray and study God's Word? Do they see you live what you preach or stand for? Do you teach them God's Word or study the bible with them?"

Excellence doesn't happen by chance or fate. It is not by accident that people choose to visit Dubai for a vacation despite the city's exceptionally high temperatures; Dubai's many beautiful attractions are the fruits of excellence derived from meticulous planning and perseverance. Great organisations don't hit and exceed their annual goals by chance. Even the conflict between Ukraine and Russia is not by chance. It is strategic. It is by preparation –

planning and acting. These entities strategise to make things work. Even the devil strategizes. Why then would you expect your children to turn out excellent by chance when the enemy is strategizing and preparing against them? 1 Peter 5: 8 (Amplified Bible) says,

> *"Be sober [well balanced and self-disciplined], be alert and cautious at all times. That enemy of yours, the devil, prowls around like a roaring lion [fiercely hungry], seeking someone to devour".*

The devil is constantly seeking who to mess with, but your strategic preparation of your child's spirit can help them stand and be courageous no matter the odds thrown at them. That child who you desire to be refined into gold, that child whom your heart delights in, that child who is God's gift to you, and whom God has put into your custody needs to be well-balanced because the devil is going to try to shake up that child. It is the devil's duty to go about seeking who to devour. But it's your duty to rise up now and guard your loins to begin the spiritual training of your child.

> *"I have told you these things, so that in Me you may have [perfect] peace. In the world you have tribulation and distress and suffering, but be courageous [be confident, be undaunted, be filled with joy]; I have overcome the world." [My conquest is accomplished, My victory abiding".*
> (John 16:33 Amplified Bible)

The question is not 'if', but 'when' their refining process (training, grooming, coaching, instructing) will be tested. The scripture above attests that there will always be challenges for all individuals (your children inclusive) to encounter, but it is the strength of their spirit within, their depth in God that will determine how they manifest the promised victory.

In the next few pages, I will be sharing a considerable chunk of my life that has made me vulnerable in the past. Sieve what you can from the information and seek out what you will do better as a parent ready to carry on the mantle of preparing their child for excellence.

I am the first of three girls. My mum is a retired teacher and boarding house mistress, while my dad is a retired administrator. As a result of my mum's profession, we lived in the staff quarters of the school where she worked. My mum is extensively accommodating and endearing, so we always had relatives and non-relatives in our house as far as I can remember. She was the 'go to person' for every one's needs.

I must say my mother is the greatest influence of my life. I am who I am today as a result of God's grace evoked by her parenting and prayers over me. My mother is a praying woman. As a teenager, I recall going with her to prayer meetings as a travel companion, though I did not understand why she was 'stressing' me, when all I would rather do is be on my bed sleeping. During summer holidays, she would pray with us, hold deliverance sessions with us, lay hands on us and anoint us. We were like her ministerial guinea pig. If she was invited to speak, we would be her first audience, because she would have practised her sermon at home by first preaching at us before she went wherever she was invited to preach. Although I sometimes got bored of this, the truth is that every of her acts (prayer, deliverance, preaching, laying on of hands, giving effortlessly, etc) impacted my life with the benefits I am now reaping. Of course, my dad supported her in her actions. God bless them both.

I got into secondary school (Federal Government College, Lagos) at age eight, as a scholar, having attained 587 out of 600 in my national common entrance exam. I was the star and joy of my family, including the extended family. My dad was so proud of me and would boast about it everywhere. At a time, my cousins, and relatives I was meeting for the first time would make my acquaintance by saying "we've heard about you… was it not you that got scholarship into secondary school?". I was that popular. Also, I was about the smallest student in my school at the time, so it wasn't unnatural for seniors to always ask me "how old are you?", my response would then be "10 years", so I don't come across as too young and not get bullied.

However, this stardom soon changed. My grades began to dwindle to the point that I was promoted on trial from JSS2 (Year 8) to JSS3 (Year 9). I could not cope well on my own with managing my studies and emotions of being away from home at the time. Eventually, I changed schools in JSS3, and moved on to the secondary school where my mum was working at the time. You might be thinking, 'why did my parents allow me to go far away from home at such a tender age? Why did they not let me go to my mum's school from the outset?'. It was their decision, and I liked it too, but what I remember is that my grades did not get better until I finished secondary school. I did not repeat any class, but I was not excelling either.

Another battle I encountered because of my grades was getting into the university. I was not passing university entrance exams enough to secure admission. Now do not assume I was not studying; I would go for night reading (night prep for boarding students), put the book in front of me, but just did not seem to understand what I was reading. And when I understood, I could not recall. I eventually got enrolled into the university for a degree at age eighteen and completed with Second Class Upper Division. The academic battle phased out as I became more knowledgeable about my position in Christ, took my stand and understood better how to approach my studies.

The other part of my childhood that made me feel vulnerable is that I was sexually abused at three different stages of my life. The first was when I was between the age of seven and nine by an uncle. I did not understand what was being done to my body until I got to about age nine towards the end of my first year in secondary school. I was able to make the act discontinue by avoid being in an enclosed placed with him until he moved out of our home.

My second experience was at age sixteen by a female family friend who I used to respect immensely. I was obviously more knowledgeable at that time and was quick to severe it.

The third was when I was raped by a cult chief in my first year in the university at age eighteen. This nearly broke me because I felt it was uncalled for and that I did not deserve such; I was neither a club nor party girl. I was just a simple naïve girl who just got into school and was in my newly rented school apartment sleeping when it happened. But I was empowered to come out of the experience's aftermath with time through the prayers and support of my parents as well as some inspiring journals I encountered during that period.

This recount is not to form a pity party nor to create paranoia, but to remind you that what you train or not train your child for will eventually be challenged at some point in their life. It is also to remind you that you do not have control over every challenge and hurdle they will face at different stages of their life, but you have control over how you prepare them to face any challenge or battle in life.

A second reason why I chose to write my childhood story is to encourage and enlighten parents to eliminate factors that could contribute to either ignorantly endangering your children or not equipping them enough for the world they are in. My parents did their best as well as they knew how to, and I remain grateful to God and them for my life, however these experiences, particularly the abuse, could have been avoided if certain factors were eliminated and if the right structures were put in place.

Above all, these experiences impacted my life mostly positively and have contributed to who I am today as I came to realise,

> 'And we know [with great confidence] that God [who is deeply concerned about us] causes all things to work together [as a plan] for good for those who love God, to those who are called according to His plan and purpose.' Romans 8:28 (Amplified Bible).

I daresay the spiritual foundation I had received prior to the experiences gave me courage and sustained me at every moment.

This is one of the reasons I've had to write this book; to inspire other people and to enlighten parents about putting structures in place for their children. Proverbs 23:23 (Amplified Bible classic Edition) says,

> "Buy the truth and sell it not; not only that, but also get discernment and judgment, instruction and understanding".

The foot note from the amplified version for this scripture notes:

> "The ancient rabbis routinely assumed "truth" to refer to the Torah (Law), and they interpreted the first part of this command to mean that a student should pay a teacher to teach him the Torah if he can find no one to teach him for free. As for the second part, they said that if the student had to pay to learn, he should not view this as grounds to charge for teaching others but should teach the Torah for free."

I have paid for the truth with my experience and gained knowledge, wisdom and understanding. I have now decided to teach others so other children need not go through what I experienced. Children do not have to be marred before they fulfil mandate. They don't have to go through bitter experiences before they can be useful in God's kingdom.

Spiritual Structures

> [3] *For though we live in the world, we do not wage war as the world does.* [4] *The weapons we fight with are not the weapons of the world. On the contrary, they have divine power to demolish strongholds.* [5] *We demolish arguments and every pretension that sets itself up against the knowledge of God, and we take captive every thought to make it*

obedient to Christ." (2 Corinthians 10: 3-5 New International Version).

¹⁰ Finally, be strong in the Lord and in his mighty power. ¹¹ Put on the full armour of God, so that you can take your stand against the devil's schemes. ¹² For our struggle is not against flesh and blood, but against the rulers, against the authorities, against the powers of this dark world and against the spiritual forces of evil in the heavenly realms. ¹³ Therefore put on the full armour of God, so that when the day of evil comes, you may be able to stand your ground, and after you have done everything, to stand. ¹⁴ Stand firm then, with the belt of truth buckled around your waist, with the breastplate of righteousness in place, ¹⁵ and with your feet fitted with the readiness that comes from the gospel of peace. ¹⁶ In addition to all this, take up the shield of faith, with which you can extinguish all the flaming arrows of the evil one. ¹⁷ Take the helmet of salvation and the sword of the Spirit, which is the word of God. 18 And pray in the Spirit on all occasions with all kinds of prayers and requests. With this in mind, be alert and always keep on praying for all the Lord's people. (Ephesians 6:10-18 New International Version)

An important truth that has been highlighted in chapter 1 is that there is a war where the lives of our children are concerned because they are the future and belong to God's kingdom. Both scriptures above attest to the fact that this warfare is spiritual and not physical, hence cannot be won with physical weapons. It cannot simply be worn with science, philosophy, logic, or art, but with spiritual weapons. More so, this battle is not with people, it is not just against the physical governments (monarchy, judiciary, legislative or executive) of this world, rather it is against the 'spiritual forces of evil in the heavenly places' – the host of demons that work to defile, destroy, harass, tempt, and enslave mankind.

This implies that apart from the power of God, all our energies combined are to no avail against the power of darkness. The word 'mighty' in NKJV is translated 'divine power' in the New International Version which means 'dynamically powerful'. This indicates that our weapons can manifest unprecedentedly and in diverse ways.

The good news in Christ is that, not only can we resist the devil's influence in our own lives, but we can destroy his influence in the lives of others, including our children. God has given us mighty weapons to counter satanic influence and activity. We must tap into that which is already available to us. We must therefore take spiritual weapons which we have been freely given by God to stand against these forces. In order to be effective in our warfare, we must know what these weapons are, and how to use them effectively.

The "weapons" God has given us include prayer, the Word of God, and worship. We must be thoroughly immersed in these if we are going to successfully fight the "good fight of faith" and teach our children to do likewise. We will be smart and put structures in place concerning our children, but most importantly, we will pray also. We will not just pray for them; we will also pray with them. We will not just pray with them and tell them to study; we will also study with them. Remember that studying not just the bible with them, but also their secular books, which helps you see things better through their eyes, and they through yours.

Be Sensitive, But Not Paranoid

My conclusions about the horrible experiences I had could be prevented are based on the seasons of life that they occurred and the family life I grew up in. The first was in my foundational phase (0 to 8 years); if you recall from chapter three on seasons to be mindful of in child development, age 0-8 is the foundational stage of one's life where the exposure and stimulation a child gets is significant to other stages of life.

My first point here is for parents to be mindful about what they directly or indirectly expose their children to. Be present and perceptive towards your child's total needs. Some parents out of care and duty to extended family, stress avoidance, and sometimes negligence, bring in people and sometimes strangers, to live with them and practically bring up their children without vetting. I am not saying you should not help people or be kind; after all kindness is one of the virtues of excellence that must be instilled in every child through modelling. So, you should be kind. However, before you bring in that maid or relative into your home, have you prayed and checked your heart (spirit) about it? One of the things I learnt from my mother-in-law is that 'nothing is too small to pray about'. How much more the matter of bringing in a third party into your home? A third party in this regard is anyone that is not the husband, wife, or child. I must say that the uncle in this story could have been anyone; it could have been a parent, teacher or family friend who is just not right spiritually. The lesson to take from this story is to pray and check your heart (spirit) continually before you expose your children to anything or anyone new, as well as, at every moment of their lives. Ephesians 6:18 (New International Version) says,

> *"And pray in the Spirit on all occasions with all kinds of prayers and requests. With this in mind, be alert and always keep on praying for all the Lord's people."*

Regardless of your faith, you must be alert (sensitive, discerning) and prayerful at all times. This scripture also says, **'with all kinds of prayers and request', implying that nothing is too big or too small to pray about.**

Next, teach your child to be courageous and bold, and to know the purpose of their body (God's temple). One of the ways you can do this is through God's Word and through building a strong relationship with your child (See chapter 5 for more on building a strong relationship). At the first encounter of abuse, I could not tell my parents, I did not have enough courage to do so, but I was able to stop the act in my own way. However, a stronger relationship between parents and child might have curbed it earlier.

Train your Child's Spirit

Training your child's spirit by creating a positive environment for them through church and bible study is good but not enough. Proverbs 22:6 says,

> *"Train up a child in the way he should go, And when he is old, he will not depart from it."*

Training is what you do to get the desired results in our children. The dictionary meaning of the verb 'train' means to equip, to instruct, to practise with. Children need to know the fundamentals of their faith (Christianity) i.e., the fundamentals of what they believe and why they believe it. This can be done through training.

Do you know that most of us operating on our current level are only here by grace, considering that the upbringing of some of us was left to chance? The kingdom of hell is not smiling when it comes to what they are preparing for this generation and upcoming ones, especially with different waves of doctrines and legislative bills being passed lately. We must consciously do better by our children, we must groom and train them spiritually.

Eli's children were sons of a prophet but were not trained in a program.

There must be a training regimen or program for the children set in place by the parents. The parents, not the church or the school are responsible for the training program. The church and school can help, but they are secondary. If we get it right in the family level by building in the children, solid value systems, the church will have less work to do. It means the church would be teaching them other things like taking territories. Deuteronomy 6:7-8 (Amplified Bible) says,

> *"You shall teach them diligently to your children [impressing God's precepts on their minds and penetrating their hearts with His truths] and shall speak of them when you sit in your house and when you walk on the road and when you lie down and when you get up. And you shall bind them as a sign on your hand (forearm), and they shall be used as bands (frontals, frontlets) on your forehead".*

The summary of this scripture is that we should teach them at every opportunity they can learn, not just during bible study. Make every event a learning opportunity.

The Word of God in a person is what speaks when under life pressures. We should look for several avenues to get God's word into them. The earlier we start, the better. When they get out there, even from age 5 as we'll see from child developmental stages, so many things would be competing for the attention of their soul.

Spiritual Program for Mining

1. Create time to meditate on scriptures with the children. e.g., sit down with them and teach them how to meditate on Psalm 23, etc. It could be daily / every other day, or just before they go to sleep. Create time for planting God's word into them.

2. Provide them their own personal devotional materials, including a bible, notes, and designate a time and location for their devotion. Go a step further by talking to them about what they learned in their devotion time. I sometimes do this when driving my daughters to school or during family prayer time at night.

3. Teach them how to pray in their understanding, then teach them why and how to pray in the spirit when you feel their age is appropriate. I think an 8-year-old child might be ready for praying in the spirit. Once

they are baptised, make a habit of praying with them regularly. You can try 10 minutes once every week and progress.

4. Both parents need to be consistent; making your words consistent with actions is very important. It is the picture that the children see that they reproduce. They reproduce what they see us do, not just what we say. What we sow in the children is what we reap.

5. Create a confession sheet tailored to the child. The child should take the confession first thing in the morning after praying and studying God's Word.

6. Pray in the spirit for them always so that as you are planting virtues in them, and watering, the seeds will be germinating too.

7. Always confess positively concerning them. Say what you want to see concerning them and how you want them to be. No matter your state of mind, never make a negative confession about your child and be quick to counter any negative remarks that anyone makes about your children. Proverbs 18:21 says

"Death and life are in the power of the tongue."

Words that proceed from the tongue can be used as a weapon to harm and destroy or as a tool to build and heal. Our words bear tremendous impact, even more as parents. So be deliberate about what you confess about that child. There are some confession tips in Supernatural Childbirth by Jackie Mize, Power of a praying parent by Stormie Omartian, and Warrior Moms Prayer Devotional by Tomi Adisa, amongst others, that can be used by any parent.

Summary of the whole matter is that parenting is a spiritual work. We must Pray and Plan for them. Pray about the schools you want them to go, pray about their friends and relationships they will keep. These prayers must begin before and continue after they are born as we certainly cannot over-pray. Also take their spiritual training program as seriously as their academic training, and even more.

CHAPTER 5

Total Mining

"Excellence, then, being of these two kinds, intellectual and moral, intellectual excellence owes its birth and growth mainly to instruction, and so requires time and experience, while moral excellence is the result of habit or custom."

— **Aristotle**

In chapter 1, I noted that mining gold is not for the feeble. I explained that mining the gold in your child would be discomforting for both you and the child. It will be discomforting for you because you will need to make certain sacrifices- sacrifice of your time, money, emotions, attitude, habits, desire, luxury, etc. You will need to parent beyond the ordinary, shake up the norm, and go the extra mile to dig out and refine the gold in your children. It will be discomforting for your children because they would be part of the work, and you are bringing them out of their comfort zone to engage in this work.

Children and adults alike prefer to stay in their comfort zones. Most babies would rather remain in the womb than be out because of the cosy nature of the womb. Everything just comes to them in womb – food, drink, play, warmth, etc. I can testify to this with my overdue babies; they both stayed in the womb for at least 41 weeks. So, bringing the child into this world is taking them out of their comfort zone. However, the good news is that children, like every individual, can stretch as far as possible to attain anything. Even better, children have more capacity to stretch and absorb than adults. So, they will not die because you train them, they will only feel some discomfort which is natural to us all.

Even though the child's mind has an extraordinary capacity to absorb information, studies have indicated that certain parts of the brain will not develop without stimulation even in their early, formative years. The neural connections of the brain, for example, get stronger each time we practise something.

Just as a sponge absorbs water and grows when it is wet, a child's brain absorbs knowledge and grows when they learn new things. Try this: put some seeds on a foam like sponge or cotton wool and keep wetting it daily or leave it soaked in water, you will notice the seeds begin to germinate and grow. After a few days of growth, you can either take the sponge or cotton wool out of water or stop wetting it, you will notice the sponge or cotton wool will dry up. The sponge or cotton wool is likened to the child's brain; the seeds likened to information they absorb; the continuous watering is the stimulation.

Any individual can learn any subject or skill they want to learn; however it takes time and practice for these connections to be strengthened. The same way you leave the sponge out of the water to dry up, the brain can cease to develop as it should. The brain can also be likened to a muscle; the more you use or exercise it the stronger it gets! This explains why we tend to forget things we learn when we do not use it. This is the concept behind having a growth mindset.

A child has the best chance to reach their full potential with proper care and stimulation. The action of gold mining with regards to parenting correlates with stimulation. Stimulation is an action that causes someone or something to become more active or enthusiastic to develop or operate. It is considered as an essential nourishment that a child needs to develop capacity. It is an enabler. It is not the quantity but the quality of stimulation in the early years that counts. Children learn from both active and passive stimulation. TV is an example of passive stimulation in most households, through which children watch the activities of others and absorb them. A child can stretch as long as they are nurtured in the right environment and with the appropriate stimulation.

Stimulating Habits

I teach English to GCSE students, and I believe analysing quotations used by writers helps to support one's points. I found the following quotes very inspiring for cultivating excellence.

"Excellence is not a skill. It is an attitude."

— Ralph Marston

"Virtues are formed in man by his doing the actions"

— Aristotle

"We are what we repeatedly do… therefore excellence is not an act, but a habit."

— **Will Durant**

In other words, Excellence is not something you do as a one-off activity. It is a way of living. It is foundational. It requires a certain philosophical approach that brilliance and inspiration alone cannot provide. It is like an operating system whose code is habit. This is true, whether we're talking about ourselves or our children.

In addition to the roles pointed out in chapter 3, let's look at some insightful habits I find useful for parents to inculcate daily in preparing the child for excellence regardless of wealth, status, or personality. With continuous practice, these insights should help to activate your child's ability and enthusiasm to stretch, develop and operate at their golden potential. However, every child is unique and might respond in their own exclusive way. So, you can approach these insights with discretion based on each child's uniqueness.

1. Be Time Conscious

One major struggle I have when it comes to excellence in my daily living is being time conscious. This is one huge tussle my husband and I had when we first got married. It was so bad I arrived late to the station for our honeymoon trip. At the time, he was working close to the train station, while I was coming from home. Since I was coming from a longer distance and was not occupied with official work, the right thing to do would have been to leave the house earlier; rather I miscalculated, and arrived about 20 minutes late, meaning he had to wait for me at the station after a long day at work. Obviously, that was a wrong start to the honeymoon .I still catch myself rushing to leave the house to get to work on time, regardless of how far or close I live from work. That tells you being late has been a personal habit, however it is unacceptable.

The morale from that story is that I still have work to do as well. Being late is unacceptable for anyone (including me) striving towards excellence. Excellence means you can be trusted to be on time and deliver on time. "The excellent person manages himself. He will not allow the environment to manage him… Be a person of excellence, not excuses" (statustown.com). Excellence is not just about brilliance, inspiration, and skill; it also entails right habits such as time management. If we want our children to be excellent, we must also be time conscious and put structures in place to help manage time. This begins with prioritising one's life and resources including time.

2. Set your priorities right

Psalms 127:2 says,

"In vain you rise early and stay up late, toiling for bread to eat—for He gives sleep to His beloved."

Do you put your children ahead of your career, extended family, religious activity (including ministry), friends and social lifestyle, or vice-versa? You do not want to end up like Eli and Samuel in the Bible who in the name of doing ministry sacrificed the wellbeing, mindset, potentials, and entirety of their children. You need to make sacrifices of your time, money, ego, lifestyle, clothing, and more for their wellbeing.

Many times, we prioritise wrongly especially where our children are concerned. We put our children after work, career, and business. I think the only subjects that should come before our children are God and our spouse, because the depth of those two relationships spills over to how we raise our children. This is especially true when you consider that these children are gifts from God, they hold a special place in God's heart and agenda, also, He alone can give wisdom without holding back when we ask.

I am not saying you should not have a life outside your children, what I am saying is that you cut down the excesses and work together to make things work. The truth is building a smooth relationship with your partner makes the work of parenting easier. Yes, your love life is important, the oil spills over from the top to the bottom, so you still need to have your own personal time, however you must make time for the children. I sometimes find myself in a grouchy mode with everyone at home when things are not smooth between my husband and me. This means the relationship I have with my husband sometimes spills over to that of my children, though it should not be. In other words, to equip and stimulate your children positively, it is important that you as a parent be in the right place too in your spirit, soul, and body. You cannot give what you don't have.

I must also say here that this work is not for one parent but for both parents (where they are both alive) It is not just a mother or father's role, parenting is for both father and mother if they are both living. The bible says in Ecclesiastes 4:9-10 that,

> *"Two people are better off than one, for they can help each other succeed. If one person falls, the other can reach out and help. But someone who falls alone is in real trouble."*

Also, Amos 3:3 says,

> *"Can two people walk together without agreeing on the direction?"*

This brings me to the point of Synergy. Put out the fire in that argument as quickly as possible because of the wellbeing (spirit, soul, and body) of your children. The children are watching, they can sense when things are not right. You and your spouse must speak the same language (one goal) and have the same voice concerning parenting your children. You cannot be saying 'A' while your partner is saying 'M'; that's a disaster about to happen. Yet this is something that children sense and some even take advantage of. Sometimes, children who know their parents are not on the same page concerning some matters, will go to the more 'agreeable' parent (a parent that does not really take a stand), the parent that will give them a 'YES' concerning a matter knowing that their other parent might likely not give consent. Even my 4-year-old is that smart! When I refuse to give her the tablet or too many snacks, she goes to her dad to ask him for the same things while I'm not there, or vice-versa, in an attempt to see if she could get what she wants. Of course, she does not get what she wants when we sing the same song. That is what being on the same page involves. Synergy!

Another area where priorities need to be set is in our financial scale of preference. What would you rather spend money on – luxury cars, clothing, partying, properties, education? May we not labour in vain.

Have you considered why wealthy parents raise their children in specific neighbourhoods? It is not just a recipe for segregation, snobbishness, or insecurity. It is a strategic move that is backed by research. The 'so called' wealthy parents raise their children in more privileged neighbourhoods to give them an advantage. And I daresay you do not have to be wealthy to do this, you only need to be driven by a purpose (gold mining) and prioritise. That's why I used the term 'so called' wealthy.

You need to be purposeful about where you live and the schools your children go to; the vicinity does magnificent things to a child's mindset. A child who only perceives positivity will breed positivity; likewise, a child who only sees negativity will emit negativity. Garbage in, Garbage out.

Another reason why you must be deliberate about choice of schools is to create a strategic network for your children. Birds of a feather flock together! I know this might be sounding 'a little' too much, but it's true. Go and research how Prince William of England, Duke of Cambridge met Catherine Middleton, how children of notable people marry each other, and the kind of schools that world leaders including UK prime ministers attended. There is so much more, and I could go on and on. I know relationships are not all about school, it could be worship places or even in awkward places, but we must be deliberate and begin to plan from now. The good news is that it's never too late to begin.

If your focus is to mine gold in your parenting, please do not simply do what is convenient for you, but do what will bring out the best in them.

So set your priorities right!

3. Plan Your Intentions For Your Children

Parenting is like an exam where you don't get the result until about 25 years after. You need to have plans for God to fulfil Psalm 20:4. Planning brings the future into the present so you can do something about it. It gives you a purpose. Plans help you to prioritise. You also need visit your plan regularly.

In life, there are no straight routes from your point of departure to where you want to go. Your plans are your expectations. If you don't have expectations, life will simply happen to you, in essence, your children.

Planning also brings harmony into your home. Have a plan as a couple, have a plan for the family (nuclear). Have a plan for your children. As a family, you need to plant and water (build and build again). Your plan should include how you intend to plant the seeds spiritually, academically, and emotionally. You will stimulate these seeds by prayer too.

Plan to put in the work and structure around your children's age range. Pay attention to your environment and to your current era. The challenges of the current era includes the internet, computer programming, sexting, radicalisation, etc. Be aware of what's happening to your children per time and acknowledge those challenges or changes.

Your plans could also include your family charter or tradition. Have values that guide you as a family. Create traditions that help you know your children better e.g., taking a walk, eating together, watching a programme together, etc. It does not have to happen every day; it could be once a week. I recently learned that eating at the table together is a time to get to know how each member of the family is doing in their personal lives. I did not have that privilege; I was taught to be quiet when eating and we hardly ate at the table growing up.

Plant, build, prepare and mine as if you will not have another chance, because you won't have this same chance. Prepare and mine as if your life depends on it because your life depends on it. Be deliberate!

Remember, it's not a question of 'if', it's a question of 'when'. What we are preparing our children for will be challenged. There will always be challenges for them to encounter. So, what are you preparing them for? How are you stimulating or protecting and fortifying them – passively or actively? Or what else is being taught them due to your negligence? Nature appals vacuum. If you do not do it, someone, or something else will.

4. Teach them to develop good relationships

There are parents whose marriages were failing who then make decisions to stay together for the sake of the kids. It is very admirable; however, it also matters that the children have good relationships with each parent and with siblings (if they have any) irrespective of their parents' marital situation. We don't want to raise broken or bent adults; rather we want them to be outstanding. It's easier to mend other things than to mend broken human beings. Broken human beings will need more divine intervention to mend.

This brings us back to the two most important subjects that we must prioritise in our lives. Prioritise your relationship with God, and with your spouse. It spills over to how you love and mentor your children. Just as you should not compare your partner with someone else, do not compare your children with other children or with their sibling (we tend to easily do this).

Teach your children to love, care, share, forgive, not yell, **by modelling**

it. This reminds me of a time my husband and I had an argument about something. At some point during the argument, we raised our voices at each other, my first daughter who was 6 years old at the time said "God is not happy when you are angry at each other. Are you and daddy making God happy right now?" Hearing this instantly put my brain into a reset mode. I immediately became calmer, apologised to her, apologised to God and apologised to my husband in front of her and told her she was right. That God would not want us to be angry with each other, that her dad and I were just trying to sort some things out, but were wrong to raise our voices at each other, and it won't happen again. That moment onwards, whenever I felt uncomfortable about something my husband has done and I start to compose my 'reprimanding' talk, I just remember my daughter's statement about God's feelings and find a better way of voicing my feelings. We also now try to have our talk out of our children's earshot.

You are not teaching them to avoid confrontations, but to handle it better by modelling it. If you want to see kindness and other excellent attributes in your children, model it. They cannot give or display what has not been deposited into them.

5. Make your children do chores

Teach them to do the dishes, lay their bed, take out the garbage, mow the lawn, do the dishes, do their laundry, etc. These are not only simply ways to make your life easier; they are also ways to make your children's lives better, too.

Julie Lythcott-Haims, a former dean at the Stanford University explains on Ted Talk when you make children do chores, they realise, "I have to do the work of life in order to be part of life." Her Harvard Grant Study revealed that children who do chores are more successful adults. It reports that children who grow up doing chores are more likely to have the skills to collaborate with other people, be more empathetic towards others and can take on tasks independently.

For the 'privileged parents', don't let your house maids do everything. If children are not doing any house chores, it means someone else is doing that for them. This means they are exempted from not just the work, but of learning that work must be done and that everyone should contribute their quota towards the advancement of any entity or unit (home, class, group and club). Making a child do house chores is a way to teach the child to be part of a cause. These are things they should learn from home, not just school, church, or clubs. Make your child do chores and see you do chores, no matter how little, and do not be that parent who is seated in the living room and would rather call on someone else who is metres away to pick the remote control or switch on the light for them. Do chores! Be up and about! It is good exercise.

Teach your children to tidy up after themselves right from when they are toddlers as mentioned in chapter 3. It goes a long way in adding to their sense of responsibility. You teach your toddler to tidy up by showing them how to do it, not by telling them, or you do it with them. Whatever you want your children to do, do it with them. For example, when I wanted my 2-year-old to tidy up, I squat to her eye level, make eye contact, and tell her "Eni let's tidy up". I start doing it, she initially hesitates, then she joins me in doing it. That's how she learned to tidy up. She then connects the words I'm saying with my actions. That's why you see the kids between 1 to 3 years copying everything the older sibling does, especially when they are close. In the same vein, if there's any habit you want your children to pick up, do it with them. They need to see you do it first.

A child might throw tantrums when you tell them to do these things. After all, who wants to spend 5 to 10 minutes doing chores when they can be watching their favourite show for the umpteenth time? Regardless, you should hold your ground rather than avoid their tears and tantrums and end up doing the chores yourself or getting someone else to do it. I know lots of parents, especially those with Obsessive Compulsive Disorder (OCD) might fall into this trap. Adults that want things done in a certain way would rather do it themselves than allow the child to mess things up. Let them mess it up! Give them the opportunity to do it! You can redo it later to soothe your compulsions, or kindly show them how you want it done, or just leave it the way they have done it as long as it is not life threatening. You won't die if it is not done your way.

Furthermore, be an 'authoritative' parent, rather than an authoritarian or a permissive one. Create a world in which your child 'grows up with a respect for authority but does not feel strangled by it'. Balance this by not being permissive. Your parenting style should not be where 'everything goes' because in real life, not everything goes. There are consequences for all actions.

"All things are allowed," you say. But not all things are good. "All things are allowed." But some things don't help anyone'. I Corinthians 10:23 (Easy-to-Read Version).

6. Train your child to inculcate a Growth Mindset

I described what growth mindset entails in Chapter 3; having the mentality to keep evolving, learning, progressing, regardless of mistakes made. As individuals, we should always have a growth mindset rather than a fixed or scarcity mindset. This is something you should also help your children to work towards by telling and showing them. I also mentioned in Chapter 3 some of my observations about my first daughter. I noticed she usually gets upset when she does not get things right especially when it comes to her art and playing the musical instruments. She would feel discouraged when she missed notes while playing the piano or when a drawing does not come out the way she wants.

To help her, I have had to use myself as an example on how I keep trying things to get better (sometimes I would even feign mistake and try again) just for her to see that we all make mistakes but must keep trying. We even had to teach her to confess the scripture Philippians 4:13 *'I can do all things through Christ which strengthens me'*. Every time she tried again, we would acknowledge and re-affirm even when the next attempt still doesn't come out right. We have got to be their champion!

Affirmation should always come from home first, not from outside. Making it happen from the outside is what opens our kids up to unnecessary vulnerable situations.

The idea is for them to keep pushing harder. You want them to view failure, which happens to all of us, as a chance to learn and grow - not as an ending. Teach them to try and not to worry about failing. In other words, keep going, keep pushing, keep stretching, and keep stimulating. A growth mindset in this realm means you also need to keep reading up on parenting to further equip yourself. While doing all these, you must try to control your level of stress, or at least control the extent to which your children perceive your stress.

7. Teach and demonstrate high educational expectations

If you want your children to behave a certain way, the most likely way to make it happen is to model it to them. If you want your kids to study, present yourself as a good role model by studying too (even if it is a novel or magazine you are reading).Don't just read to them, read with them; this is how I taught my toddler to read. Encourage reading by having books, magazines, and newspapers in the house. Let them see you and other family members reading.

You need to have intellectual discussions with your children regularly and to do this, you need to read. You need to read and be a step ahead except you want your credibility to be questioned. You do not want to be caught saying letters of the English Alphabet starts with U, except you are trying to make a statement or joke out of it.

Your children cannot always see you watching movies or football, and you expect them to just take your word "go and study your books, no TV for you" very seriously. You will just be a joker to them. Every time you are out the door, they are on the television, and once you are almost back or they hear the hoot of your car, they flee to their rooms pretending they are reading. No, that can't work!

There was a time (a habit we need to pick up again), my husband would turn off the TV after we had all watched our last soap for the day at 9pm, pray and tell us all to pick up a book to read. Most times, someone like me would sleep off while on the 1st page; my sleeping off while reading was not the best, but an effort was made. As parents, you must make effort and find strategies that work for you as a family. You cannot afford to leave these things to chance or to other people (school, clubs).

Have family rules and consistently stick with them. We cannot be permissive – where anything goes. Have timetables for them (separate for school time and holiday), so they are not always on TV or playing games. Even adults need to plan their time, how much more children. A couple of summers ago, we created a food and activity timetable we had been procrastinating about for the kids and realised it was rewarding, even for us parents. We did not have to bother about what they would eat per time or about their activities. It makes life easier and helps you develop time management and organisational skills in them. The older one knows what's on the timetable better than I who made it and she used to remind me of what was on her timetable.

Get your children positively excited about 'difficult' subjects like Mathematics from an early stage. You can start reading to your child from 6 months or earlier. Check out Glenn Doman's book on 'How to teach your baby to read'. Research physical games, toys and books that can help to spark up children's interests in academics - Snakes and Ladder, Qwirkle, and Sum Swamp board games are good for Maths whilst Scrabble, Hangman and Charades are great examples for English. Please try to sit with them when they are learning or playing games. Let them see you are interested. Even if they have lesson teachers or tutors, try to listen in; it is not about trust issues, you can also help solve some of the questions if they have problems solving them later on their own. Don't be an absent parent or come across as unintelligent. Even if you make mistakes while solving the question together, it's part of growth mindset.

Furthermore, observe the interests of your child from their early childhood years. Encourage them to scribble or draw; let them make marks. It is a functional skill for writing. If you notice that your child likes scribbling or drawing, give them paper and pencil or crayon, let them scribble and draw all they want. Then go a step further by asking them about what they've drawn. Talk about the image or lines they have put on paper. As soon as you discover your child's strengths, get them to practise it more, stimulate as much as possible. They could be better than James Gosling, Walt Disney, Tiger Woods, Mo Farah, Serena Williams, and much more.

If you notice they like to tear down and build up, give them toys that can stimulate and build up those skills like Lego and stacking cups. We nicknamed my second daughter 'engineer' because we noticed in her first year that she liked to dismantle things and try putting them back together. So, we started engaging her more with toys and activities that related to building and construction. Just endeavour to engage them actively and positively. If you don't engage them, they will find an alternative to engage themselves which might be counterproductive.

Finally, share your personal education experiences and goals with your children and prompt them to have educational goals they can also share with you. It makes you and them particularly, feel accountable to each other. My daughter asks about the progress I am making with any assignment I might have, including progress with this book, and vice-versa. Sometimes I pick up the work because I know she would ask; that accountability keeps me in check. Finally, celebrate family and individual achievements of yourselves and the children. Give reward for good behaviour, not bribe them.

8. Teach them the concept of hard work (Work Ethics and Achievement)

There are three quotients you should help your child develop beyond intelligence. They are Emotional Quotient (EQ), Social Quotient (SQ), and Adversity Quotient (AQ). EQ is an individual's ability to regulate their emotions in daring times, while SQ is a measure of a person's ability to build a network of friends and maintain it over a long period of time. We have elaborated quite well on the emotional and social quotients using Erikson's theory in chapter 3; adversity intelligence is also important.

Adversity Quotient (AQ) is a score that measures the ability of a person to handle adversities in their life. It is also likened to terms such as resilience, tenacity, and persistence. It is the capacity to bounce back when you have been pushed down. Individuals with strong AQ are tough and will not wallow in self-pity when life deals roughly. Such a person will not easily give up in the face of setbacks. People with high AQ have a positive attitude to life easily, adapt to changes, and are more able to regulate their emotions. Proverbs 24:10 says,

> "If you faint in the day of adversity, Your strength is small". I like the way the Message translation puts it, "If you fall to pieces in a crisis, there wasn't much to you in the first place."

Oops…

How can gold that has been mined through the hottest fire not be able to withstand other pressures and crisis that life throws? An excellent child must be able to withstand pressures, crisis, and other unfriendly conditions. Having a crisis is not what matters, rather it is how it is handled, and remember the best way to teach children is by how you also respond to adverse conditions.

Know when a child is acting up and when they are certainly stressed or cannot go further. I have seen and heard young children say, "I am stressed", "I am depressed", at the slightest adverse condition, even before Covid-19 ever happened. I am not inhibiting the impact of one's mental health, however I have observed children, especially from more privileged backgrounds find it hard to cope in adverse situations. This indicates that children are not being stretched as much as they should, another reason why they should do house chores.

Teach your children adversity quotient. Teach them to be strong. From their mid-teenage years (14-16 years), they can begin to do holiday jobs, not just for the money but to acquire tenacity and understand work ethic and achievement. They don't need to be graduates to get their first job or gig. These are efforts that need to be put into excellence. Esther's uncle 'Mordecai' and Daniel understood the place of season, gift, personal effort (Daniel 1:4, Esther 2:2). They understood that being beautiful, handsome, gifted, or/and talented is not enough to produce excellent results. Daniel let go of meat and other specialties his peers were having. Likewise Esther, she fasted (deprived) herself of what she should normally have because she was fighting for a cause. Give your children responsibilities. Stretch them at home, give them intellectual, emotional, physical and spiritual tasks, stimulate them, and give them opportunities to go through the refining process.

Financial intelligence is another skill you want to equip them with as you teach them the concept of hard work. Teach them to save and handle money correctly. When you send your child on errands that involve money, keep them accountable to provide the balance of their transactions. Encourage the early use of piggybanks and safe deposit boxes. Additionally, teach them about modern financial tools through books such as: Grandpa's Fortune Fables: Fun stories to teach kids about money, My First Book about Financial Education: How to save money and make it grow, Rich Dad Poor Dad for Kids, Think and Grow Rich for Children, amongst others.

9. Teach them social skills.

A 20-year research on children at Duke University and Pennsylvania State University indicate that children with good social skills turned out to be more successful. It is also said that success is 20% competence and 80% relationships (subject to profession and career level). That suggests the significance of social skills to success. In recent times, one's ability to excel in many environments thrive on the ability to be socially competent – to sustain discussions, to cooperate with peers without prompting, be helpful to others, understand others' feelings, and resolve problems. One person I know who has strong social quotient is my husband; his ability to build a network of friends and maintain it over a long period of time is amazing and inspiring. I hope he can instil the same in our children, and I pray to do better too.

Exposure has made me realise that social skills is tantamount to respect and that respect is not about avoiding eye contact or not being able to look at someone (an adult) at eye level during conversations as we were traditionally taught. In fact, it is the exact opposite.

Teach your children to respond to compliments and extend compliments too. 'What's good for the goose is good for the gander'. Teach them to reciprocate and initiate kindness and empathy. Teach them to share (toys inclusive), and to use the magic words (please, thank you, excuse me, pardon me), and more from the early stage. Proverbs 22:6 (New International Version) says,

> "Start children off on the way they should go, and even when they are old, they will not turn from it".

Remember teaching is not just telling, it is by modelling it. This is a call for parents to be extra kind to members of the family and people outside the household. You are passing by, and you see a familiar face, say hello; this is teaching your children to greet as well. You won't then need to say, "can't you greet?". Children do not learn by mere words but by precepts. You want your children to do something for you, use 'please' and 'thank you' for the errands. Don't practise some of the not-so-good habits of your parents - that has got to stop with us.

As parents, we should do better. Teach your children to gracefully fit into wherever they find themselves socially and intellectually, of course without losing the God-inspired values you have inculcated in them. Adjust your culture at home to suit your expectations for your children's future lifestyle so your children won't find it too difficult to adjust to the culture outside the home. For example, if you expect your children to go to proper (posh) schools where children eat in the hall with proper cutleries during lunch, or to meet and socialise with people of a particular standard, teach them to practise these things at home. This is an addendum to the guides given at the autonomy vs. shame and doubt stage. Remember, they are arrows in your hands, they represent you. Do not let them depend on the outside world for the changes they need to effect from the inside. This is a call to duty for you and me.

Still talking about social skills, prayerfully teach your kids to be bold and confident. This is one area I am trusting God for. I grew up quite timid, and I don't want my children to be that way. My summary of Psalms 127: 3-5 is that a parent who has his quiver full of children that have been prepared as arrows is blessed. Opponents and accusers don't stand a chance because these children will represent judiciously. I don't want to raise children that cannot stand up for themselves or even me when I am not there.

An example I will cite here is about a family friend who recently got off a major financial mess that affected their family's ability to pay their children's fees. She told me of how her 8-year-old daughter stood up for herself in school. Due to the financial mess they faced, the child could not attend school for about 3 weeks because they had been owing fees for about 3 months. Because of the girl's absence from school, other pupils in the class and parents had started to gossip about the financial state of this family. By the time the child returned to school, one of the girl's classmates was silly enough to make fun of the girl to her face, about not being able to afford school fees. It was very impressive to know that the girl did not cringe at the other girl's taunting comments; rather she responded in the summarised words, "do you know what my parents have been through? Even if my parents cannot pay, what business of yours is it?" At the end of the day, the other girl felt embarrassed and dumbfounded and said "well, don't stress me". That ended the matter. My 8-year-old family friend could have handled the situation differently by reporting to a teacher or respond aggressively, but she chose to stand up for herself and family, she understood what she represented (her family) and handled it well. She is still friends with the other girl now, after 4 years.

We must teach our children to be bold and hold their head high, make decisions and be ready to take responsibility for those decisions.

10. Be your children's best friends

Another lesson I took from the above story is that the parents of the 8-year-old girl did not hide their financial state from the child. They shared it with her, equipped (worked with) her to understand the situation and possibly how to rise above it. Their sharing the information with her, making constant positive declarations and confessions as a family also made her feel part of something that would get better. She felt RESPONSIBLE.

Please share real life-experiences with your children appropriately and with the right motives; not out of anger or fear, but to 'prepare' them for an excellent future.

I remember that one of the facts that positively contributed to my decision to avoid a wayward lifestyle in the university was because of personal experiences my mum had shared with me while younger. I did not really get the 'if you stand close to a man, you'll get pregnant' kind of lecture. I already knew as a young child that I was conceived outside wedlock (I wasn't told in a malicious way, it was more like a gist), so I made up my mind even early in life that it was not going to happen to me.

Your child(ren) should feel comfortable enough to come to you and talk with you about anything. Let your child come to understand that they can be vulnerable with you and move on. Prepare them to know that you won't use any secrets or information they divulge to you against them. Boldly and lovingly say 'I love you' to them irrespective of their gender and mean it. Don't wait for someone to tell them outside. Do the homework now while you can, soon they would be out of your air and space. This is the time for action.

I once watched a movie where a mother reprimanded her husband for being nice and playful with their child; she said to him "you can't be a father and friend all at once to your child". That took me aback and I felt '……mmm, whose terms? Who would you rather be your child's first friend – the person waiting to take advantage of them outside?

Sincerely, I think the solution to this statement is that we need to balance things. I believe you can actually be your children's parent and friend at the same time. It's best we are first their friends before they begin to have other friends outside (which they certainly will). Our friendship with them and values we have inculcated over time will go a long way to prepare them in their choice of friends, politeness to friends and how they handle relationships generally.

Speak to your children as friends, not as a commander of the army. However, you should create positive relations and enforce rules without focusing always on punishment.

Finally, parents should have conversations with children. I cannot overstress this. Sexual education for your child should not first occur in school but at home, between a child and parent. Note I did not say mother/father, but parent. Children should know the functions of their body parts at an early age. I daresay not later than age 5, children should know their body parts that nobody besides them should touch. Age 5 is significant because at this stage, most children need less personal care. For instance at this age, most children can clean up after themselves when they wee or poo, especially if parents and / or caregivers have been teaching them to be independent from the toddler stage. Another reason why this stage of development is critical is that this is the age where they begin to make up their own rules, where children begin to determine who to play with or who not to play with, and the type of play or activity to engage in. When a child at this stage understands simple boundaries including their body boundaries, they would be in a better place to refuse any unwarranted and unwanted touch.

CONCLUSION

There is no such thing as a complete list. The most important key to attaining excellence at any stage is to have a growth mindset towards raising our children and towards life generally. Again, excellence is a continuous process, and thus, it is a habit. If there's any habit you want to see in your children, you should model it to them by exhibiting the same and/or doing it with them. They need to see you do it first.

Be actively involved in the development of your child's spirit, soul, and body. The work should not be left to the school, nanny, house-help, church, clubs, friends, or children themselves. Do not leave the development of your children to people other than themselves. Let your voice of reasoning, peace, kindness, love, compassion, justice, virtue and honour be the loudest in their hearts.

Set boundaries by creating some sort of schedule. Children might want to push these boundaries, but you should stand your ground. Do not ever give empty threats. Set boundaries and be consistent in following through with consequences.

Remember our anchor scripture in Psalms 127 instructing us not to toil aimlessly, hence sacrificing the child on the altar of toiling and trying to make ends meet. Also recall the parable of the talent in the Bible, how God rewarded each custodian according to how well they worked on their gifts. That child is the gift that God has given you to look after. Set your priorities right so that after all is said and done, God who gave you the child can say to you "well done good and faithful servant, enter into your rest". May we not toil in vain in Jesus' name.

Finally, enjoy where you are on the way to where you are going.

Much love,

Tosin Oke

FURTHER RESOURCES

Other online resources and activities I can recommend especially for children at nursery & primary levels are:

https://www.bbc.co.uk/bitesize/topics/zjkphbk/articles/zf4sscw

https://www.bbc.co.uk/cbeebies/topics/numeracy

https://www.mathplayground.com/

https://home.oxfordowl.co.uk/kids-activities/fun-maths-games-and-activities/v

https://www.youtube.com/watch?v=CyElHdaqkjo

CONTACT US

For prayers or any enquiries, you can contact me via email at goldmining@gmail.com and on Instagram @gracefuloaks_GM.

REFERENCES

British Broadcasting Coporation. (2022). Bitesize. Available at: https://www.bbc.co.uk/bitesize/topnics/zjkphbk/articles/zf4sscw [Accessed July 1, 2022].

British Broadcasting Corporation. (2022). CBeeies. Available at cbeeies.com: https://www.bbc.co.uk/cbeebies/topics/numeracy [Accessed March 18, 2022].

California Department of Education. (2000). Ages and Stages of Development. Available at cde.ca.gov: https://www.cde.ca.gov/SP/CD/re/caqdevelopment.asp [Accessed on May 18, 2022].

Cambridge University Press. (2021). Cambridge Dictionary. Available at: https://dictionary.cambridge.org [Accessed on July 18, 2022].

Centre for Disease Prevention and Control (2022). CDC Developmental Milestones. Available at cdc.gov: https://www.cdc.gov/ncbddd/actearly/milestones/index.html [Accessed on April 1, 2022].

Cherry, Kendra. (2020). Stages of Prenatal Development. Available from verywellmind.com: https://www.verywellmind.com/stages-of-prenatal-development-2795073 [Accessed on April 12, 2022].

Cherry, Kendra. (2022). Erikson's Stages of Development: A Closer Look at the Eight Psychosocial Stages. Available at verywellmind.com: https://www.verywellmind.com/erik-eriksons-stages-of-psychosocial-development-2795740 [Accessed on April 20, 2022].

King, Collen. (2002). Math Playground. Available from mathplayground.com: https://www.mathplayground.com/ [Accessed on June 18, 2022].

Merriam-Webster. (1828). Meriam-Webster's Dictionary. Available at Merriam-webster.com: https://www.merriam-webster.com [Accessed on July 18, 2022].

Montessori, M. (1995). The Absorbent mind (1st ed.). Henry Holt: New York.

Oxford University Press. (2022). Oxford Owl. Available at Oxford Owl for Home: https://home.oxfordowl.co.uk/kids-activities/fun-maths-games-and-activities/v [Accessed on March 18, 2022].

Parenting First Cry (2022). Foetal Brain Developmental Stages and Foods to Improve Development. Available from parentingfirstcry.com: https://parenting.firstcry.com/articles/fetal-brain-development-stages-and-foods-to-improve-development/ [Accessed on May 18, 2022].

Tassoni, P. (2013). BTEC First Children's Play, Learning and Development. Pearson: UK.

Webster's New World College Dictionary (2010) Arete. 4th Ed. Houghton Mifflin Harcourt. Cited in Collin's Dictionary. (Accessed 22/6/2022)

BOOK REVIEW

'Gold Mining - Parenting an Excellent Child' was written with full dedication and passion. This book proves she has a wealth of knowledge in the world of parenting through her career.

As an educator and author, I have seen that the world is getting busier, and it is affecting good parenting. There are quite a lot of things competing for the time of both parents and children so nurturing and rearing children has become increasingly difficult. Children cannot be raised in your spare time the same way flowers need to be nurtured in order to bloom. I am hopeful that this book will impact readers' minds to new perspectives; helping them to understand their child in a new way and truly make them a gold mine.

— **Olubusola Kolade**
Founder, Ornaments of Grace, and Virtue (OGAV)

•••

Only God can count the number of apples in a seed, this is the story of potential. Tosin has written a fantastic book on the subject of parenting – a subject that is close to my heart - in a balanced way not leaning too heavily on just one side. This is a guide that if followed, will truly help the reader mine the best outcome from children. The content is complete, and it has a good academic slant which shows that the author studied and has a basis for the things she has written.

Tosin has also put some good real-life examples to show that she is living what she is teaching. This is the first of more to come from her. Enjoy and be expectant

I pray this book becomes a best seller, best read and best used book of wisdom.

Kudos, Tosin!

— **Ola Lekan Fasina**
Founder, Treasures in Clay, Int'l

•••

EDITOR'S REMARKS

I would like to say that your work is a treasure, and I have been blessed through this process. Thank you.

∙∙∙

Printed in Great Britain
by Amazon